What's That Supposed To Mean?

Using The Catechism In The 21st Century

James A. Lucas

CSS Publishing Company, Inc., Lima, Ohio

WHAT'S THAT SUPPOSED TO MEAN?

Copyright © 2000 by
CSS Publishing Company, Inc.
Lima, Ohio

All rights reserved. No part of this publication may be reproduced in any manner whatsoever without the prior permission of the publisher, except in the case of brief quotations embodied in critical articles and reviews. Inquiries should be addressed to: Permissions, CSS Publishing Company, Inc., P.O. Box 4503, Lima, Ohio 45802-4503.

Some scripture quotations are from the *Holy Bible, New International Version.* Copyright © 1973, 1978, 1984 International Bible Society. Used by permission of Zondervan Bible Publishers. All rights reserved.

Some scripture quotations are from the *Revised Standard Version of the Bible,* copyrighted 1946, 1952 ©, 1971, 1973, by the Churches of Christ in the USA. Used by permission.

Library of Congress Cataloging-in-Publication Data

Lucas, James A., 1953-
    What's that supposed to mean? : using the catechism in the 21st century / James A. Lucas.
       p.   cm.
    Includes bibliographical references.
    ISBN 0-7880-1564-8 (pbk. : alk. paper)
    1. Luther, Martin, 1483-1546. Kleine Katechismus. 2. Lutheran Church — Doctrines — Sermons. 3. Church year sermons. 4. Sermons, American. I. Title: What is that supposed to mean?. II. Title.
BX8070.L8 L73   2000
252'.041—dc21   99-052801

This book is available in the following formats, listed by ISBN:
   0-7880-1564-8   Book
   0-7880-1565-6   Disk
   0-7880-1566-4   Sermon Prep

PRINTED IN U.S.A.

*Dedicated to
my wife Denise,
the people of Redeemer Lutheran Church, Wauneta Nebraska,
the people of Trinity Lutheran Church, Palisade, Nebraska,
who listened to these sermons first,
and to the Reverend Dr. Paul Johnston,
friend, counselor, and sage who rode herd on this project*

Sections of Luther's *Small Catechism* are reproduced from *Dr. Martin Luther's Small Catechism,* © 1943 by Concordia Publishing House. Used by permission of Concordia Publishing House.

The quotation by Sherwood Wirt is reproduced from *Illustrations for Biblical Preaching.* Edited by Michael P. Green. Foreword by Haddon W. Robinson. Grand Rapids, Michigan: Zondervan Publishing Company, 1990, pp. 57-58. Copyright © HarperCollins Publishers, 1990. Used by permission of HarperCollins Publishers.

The quotation by C. S. Lewis is reproduced from *Mere Christianity,* copyright © C. S. Lewis Pte. Ltd, 1952. Extracts used by permission.

Table Of Contents

Foreword 9
   Dr. A. L. Barry, President
   The Lutheran Church — Missouri Synod

Introduction 11
   Dr. Arthur A. Just, Jr., Professor
   Concordia Theological Seminary
   Fort Wayne, Indiana

Preface 17
   Dr. David P. Scaer, Professor
   Concordia Theological Seminary
   Fort Wayne, Indiana

Author's Preface 21

The Ten Commandments
1. The First Commandment:
   Eyes On Jesus — 23
2. The Second Commandment:
   God's Name — 27
3. The Third Commandment:
   Holding God's Word Sacred — 31
4. The Fourth Commandment:
   Holding Parents In Love And Esteem — 35
5. The Fifth Commandment:
   Help And Befriend — 39
6. The Sixth Commandment:
   A Chaste And Decent Life — 43
7. The Seventh Commandment:
   Improve And Protect — 47
8. The Eighth Commandment:
   Speak Well Of Your Neighbor — 51
9. The Ninth Commandment:
   Help And Be Of Service — 55

10. The Tenth Commandment: Satisfaction	59
11. The Close Of The Commandments: Grace And Every Blessing	63

The Apostles' Creed

12. The First Article: God Gave Me My Eyes And Ears	67
13. The First Article: God Provides For Me	71
14. The First Article: God's Fatherly, Divine Goodness And Mercy	75
15. The First Article: My Duty To Thank And Praise	79
16. The Second Article: Begotten Of The Father From Eternity	83
17. The Second Article: Jesus Born Of The Virgin Mary Is My Lord	87
18. The Second Article: Jesus Is My Lord	91
19. The Second Article: Jesus Christ Redeemed Me	95
20. The Second Article: Lost And Condemned	99
21. The Second Article: Jesus Purchased And Won Me	103
22. The Second Article: Protected From The Devil's Power	107
23. The Second Article: A New Purpose In Life	111
24. The Second Article: God's Power Takes Care Of Me	115
25. The Second Article: Risen From The Dead	119
26. The Second Article: What Jesus Does For Us Today	123
27. The Third Article: Called By The Gospel	127

28. The Third Article:
    Enlightened With His Gifts   131
29. The Third Article:
    Sanctified And Kept In Faith   135
30. The Third Article:
    He Calls, Gathers, Enlightens The Whole Church   139
31. The Third Article:
    Rich And Daily Forgiveness   143
32. The Third Article:
    Raise Up Me And All The Dead   147
33. The Third Article:
    God's Gift Of Eternal Life   151

The Lord's Prayer

34. The Introduction:
    Our Father In Heaven   155
35. The First Petition:
    Hallowed Be Thy Name   159
36. The Second Petition:
    Thy Kingdom Come   163
37. The Third Petition:
    Thy Will Be Done   167
38. The Fourth Petition:
    Give Us This Day Our Daily Bread   171
39. The Fifth Petition:
    Forgive Us Our Trespasses   175
40. The Sixth Petition:
    Lead Us Not Into Temptation   179
41. The Seventh Petition:
    Deliver Us From Evil   183
42. The Conclusion:
    Thine Is The Kingdom   187
43. The Conclusion:
    Thine Is The Power   193
44. The Conclusion:
    Thine Is The Glory   197
45. The Conclusion:
    Amen   203

The Sacrament Of Holy Baptism
46. Holy Baptism:
    Washed In God's Name ... 207
47. Holy Baptism:
    A Bath That Renews ... 211

The Office Of The Keys And Confession
48. The Office Of The Keys:
    Why Pastors? ... 215
49. Confession:
    Confess And Absolve ... 221

The Sacrament Of The Altar
50. The Sacrament Of The Altar:
    Given For You ... 225
51. The Sacrament Of The Altar:
    Eat And Drink Forgiveness ... 229
52. The Sacrament Of The Altar:
    The Worthy Dinner Guest ... 233

Appendix
Hymns For Use With Sermons ... 237

Foreword

As I reviewed the 52 devotional sermons on Luther's *Small Catechism* that Pastor Lucas has prepared, I was impressed by the quality. I can well imagine a congregation and its pastor making use of these sermons to delve more deeply into the treasures of the *Small Catechism*.

I certainly do pray for God's richest blessings on all those who will make use of this important collection of sermons.

A. L. Barry, President
The Lutheran Church — Missouri Synod
St. Louis, Missouri

Introduction

Catechesis. This is a strange word to many people today, but there is a growing awareness of its meaning and its significance. It has a long and venerable history stretching back to the gospel of Luke and beyond that to the book of Deuteronomy. Luke the evangelist writes to Theophilus a narrative of events from the life of Jesus that are intended to proclaim to him the reality of Jesus' death and resurrection and its meaning for his life. Luke puts it this way: "It seemed good to me also, after investigating from the beginning every tradition carefully, to compose systematically a narrative for your benefit, most excellent Theophilus, in order that you come to recognize completely the reliability of the words by which you have been catechized" (Luke 1:3-4).

Catechesis! Luke uses this strange word to describe for Theophilus the purpose of his Gospel — Luke writes to give Theophilus certainty concerning the teachings about Jesus he had received, that is, his catechesis.

What does this mean? Martin Luther's *Small Catechism* asks this question over and over again as it wrestles with the central doctrines of the faith, and it is still a good question to ask today. What does catechesis mean? It comes from the Greek word for "echo," and it describes the process of teaching that takes place between the teacher and his hearers. The teacher speaks and the hearer "echoes" back what he hears. But in catechesis, the teaching is so taken to heart that the "echo" is both heard and seen, for the hearer shows his understanding of the teaching by what he says and what he does. The whole person is affected by this teaching so that after hearing catechesis, one is never the same again. Catechesis transforms lives because the Word that is taught is God's Word, and this Word brings people into communion with Jesus Christ by the power of the Holy Spirit.

Catechesis, that is, teaching about Jesus Christ that transforms lives and brings people into communion with Jesus, is recorded in books called catechisms. Luther's *Small Catechism* has endured for over 460 years as the primary means of teaching the biblical faith to children and adults in the Lutheran Church. Even today it is the standard text in confirmation classes across the world. Since the Reformation, the Lutheran Church has maintained a strong catechetical tradition, and even churches that do not bear the name "Lutheran" use Luther's *Small Catechism* because it contains the essence of the Christian faith in six chief parts that are simple and easy to teach to children and adults alike: The Ten Commandments, The Apostles' Creed, The Lord's Prayer, The Sacrament of Holy Baptism, The Office of the Keys and Confession, and The Sacrament of the Altar.

Luther's *Small Catechism* was written to be heard and memorized. One thing that should not be done with the catechism is to turn it into a syllabus to be used exclusively in a classroom where the Christian faith is taught like math or science or social studies. The catechism is to be prayed and preached, for the words it contains are living words that bring to the hearer a life that does not end. Catechesis does not convey facts about God, but instead offers to the hearer a person who invaded our world from heaven, sat at our tables and taught us about our Father in heaven, allowed himself to be nailed to a tree outside Jerusalem on a Friday we now call Good, burst the bonds of death on the third day, and ascended back to heaven on the fortieth. As we hear in catechesis what God has done for us, we echo back our affirmation of his work in our confession of faith and in our charitable lives because Christ now dwells in us by his Word and Spirit, and we are now children of the heavenly Father in Christ. And as Saint Paul says: "And because you are sons, God has sent forth the Spirit of His Son into your hearts, crying out, 'Abba Father!' " (Galatians 4:6).

The best place for catechesis is in the church gathered for worship, for this is where Jesus has promised to be present in his flesh by Word and Spirit. As we assemble together as Christ's saints, we enter into an ongoing life of catechesis where the Lord Jesus is our teacher. He teaches us through his Word and then offers his body and blood in, with, and under bread and wine. The pastor stands in Christ's stead and by his command, and when we hear him read Scripture and preach the gospel and offer us the gift of the Lord's Supper, he is doing this because Christ has called him to serve the people of God as his representative. The pastor is offering us Christ in Word and Sacrament, and he does this catechetically, that is, he speaks and we listen, and then we speak back to him what we have heard in our confession of sin and our confession of faith, in hymns of praise and prayers of thanksgiving. This rhythm of speaking and hearing and responding is devotional as we meditate on what we hear, and respond with love and affection to the One who first loved us.

The preaching of the Word is that moment in our worship where the pastor announces to us what it all means. He does not intend simply to teach but declares to us that what we are hearing is real because it is about a person who is real, and who is present among us as our crucified and risen Lord. In the sermon, the pastor takes the Word of God that we have heard and he applies it to our lives; that is, he brings Christ to us by announcing that the gifts of life, salvation, and forgiveness are ours because Christ is offering them to us right here and now in the very preaching of his Word. Like John the Baptist, the pastor prepares us to receive the gifts by calling us to repentance and faith, and then as Jesus' representative he forgives us our sins, proclaims Christ's rescue of creation from its enemies of sin, death, and devil, and then offers the new eternal life Jesus obtained when he conquered death. This new life is now dwelling in us because Jesus Christ is dwelling in us. In the preaching of the Word the pastor addresses our question "What does this mean?" by telling us that the meaning may be found in the life, death, and resurrection of Jesus Christ of Nazareth.

In this book Pastor James A. Lucas provides us with sermons that offer real life in Jesus Christ by confronting that tough question that God's people want addressed: "What does this mean?" By systematically preaching through the entire *Small Catechism* of Martin Luther, Pastor Lucas speaks as a pastor to his people, and as their pastor he knows that the most important thing he must do is bring them into communion with Jesus Christ. His sermons clearly explain the meaning of each part of the catechism, illustrate that meaning with incisive and relevant examples, and then point the hearer to Jesus Christ who is central to every sermon. The rhythm of Law and Gospel is present in every sermon with every kind of clarity and forcefulness that people today are yearning for in preaching.

Pastor Lucas follows in the footsteps of Martin Chemnitz, who in his catechetical book *Ministry, Word, and Sacraments: An Enchiridion* says that to preach the gospel, one preaches Christ. In the devotional sermons offered here, Christ is preached as the One who came from heaven into our world to bear our sicknesses and infirmities and release us from our captivity to a lost and fallen world. Here you will hear not only what Jesus Christ has done, but you will discover who he is as the incarnate Son of God, how he entered into our ordinary lives, walked with us on our roads, came into our homes to heal our sick, to teach us about his Father and about himself, and then take his final, lonely journey to a cross planted outside the city. And here Pastor Lucas will show you that because the tomb is empty, you now live in a creation that is new and restored and that is waiting with expectation and groaning for Jesus to come again.

These sermons are easy to use. The format is clean and simple. Each sermon begins with a title that includes a section of the *Small Catechism* and a theme for the sermon. Then Pastor Lucas provides three Scripture texts that are related to this part of the catechism, with one text highlighted as the primary source of his devotion. Highlighted in a box is the portion of the catechism under consideration. What follows is his devotional sermon that carefully connects catechism and Scripture to illustrate in a pastoral way how Christ is speaking to us about who he is and who we are because of him. Each section closes with a prayer that reflects the themes of the devotional sermon, providing a fitting conclusion to each section. Some sections also include an object lesson that provides an opportunity for the pastor or teacher (or parent) to illustrate the catechism for children. An appendix suggests four hymns to be used with each sermon with the numbers given from both *The Lutheran Hymnal* and *Lutheran Worship*.

What you have before you is a delightful excursion into the mysteries of the faith as Luther presented them in the *Small Catechism*, and as Pastor Lucas now presents them in these 52 devotional sermons. These sermons are for pastors and teachers and laity alike. Read them as they were written to be read — pastor speaking to his flock about life in Jesus Christ.

It is a privilege to introduce this work by Pastor Lucas — my classmate from seminary, my colleague in the ministerium and my friend — to the church at large, and to commend this valuable contribution to the congregational life of our churches.

Then Jesus said to them, "These are the words which I spoke to you while I was still with you, that all things must be fulfilled which were written in the Law of Moses and the Prophets and the Psalms concerning Me." And he opened their understanding, that they might comprehend the Scriptures. Then he said to them, "Thus it is written, and thus it was necessary for the Christ to suffer and to rise from the dead the third day, and that repentance and remission of sins should be preached in his name to all nations, beginning at Jerusalem. And you are witnesses of these things."
— Luke 22:44-48

Arthur A. Just, Jr.
Feast of Saint Luke, 1998

Preface

One challenge Lutheran pastors face is keeping their congregations Lutheran in an environment in which confessional loyalties have less importance. People moving from one place to another often choose churches not because of their denominational affiliation, but because of their programs. What this or that church officially believes and actually teaches — these are often different — is sometimes not a pressing factor in choosing church membership. So pastors confront two problems. Members who were baptized and confirmed as Lutherans must be fortified in what they believe, since they can easily be attracted to other churches. Pastors know that a course covering several months is not really long enough to do the job for those who have chosen the Lutheran church in their adult years. Martin Luther did not face the problem of converts who needed reinforcement in the faith. His job was, however, at least as difficult or even more so than ours. During the early years of the Reformation he had to bring the people from a medieval understanding of Christianity to an evangelical understanding of it, but he was determined to preserve its catholic or ecumenical core. What better way than to set down the evangelical faith around the Ten Commandments, the Apostles' Creed, and the Lord's Prayer.

Before the Lutherans set down their faith in the Augsburg Confession in 1530, Luther saw his Reformation threatened by the Anabaptists who denied the Trinity and the Baptism of infants and by Ulrich Zwingli, the first of a long line of Reformed theological leaders who refused to identify the bread and wine of the Lord's Supper with Christ's body and blood. Unless the ordinary people were kept from these false teachings and won for the Reformation, Luther's cause would be lost. To win the hearts of the people and to lead them into the newly-discovered faith, Luther prepared the *Small* and *Large Catechisms* in 1529. By then twelve years had elapsed since he had nailed the now famous *Ninety-Five Theses* to the door of the Castle Church in Wittenberg, at whose university he was a professor of theology and where he served with his friend

Johann Bugenhagen as a pastor of Saint Mary's Church. The *Large Catechism* was a collection of sermons, and like the *Small Catechism* was included in the *Book of Concord* which Lutherans revere as their confessions, that is, statements of their faith. No other Christian group gives their doctrinal statements such a high place. Whereas Luther's sermons which became the *Large Catechism* are no longer preached, the *Small Catechism*, often taught to children for their confirmation, has remained the staple of Lutheran church life for nearly five centuries. It is a classic in its own right.

By organizing a complete series of sermons based on the *Small Catechism* for the 52 Sundays of the year, the Reverend James Lucas, a pastor in The Lutheran Church — Missouri Synod now serving in Elkhart, Kansas, is bringing to life Luther's seminal work for Lutheran congregations at the dawn of the twenty-first century. Luther intended his catechism to be immediately usable by the people and accessible to them so that the profound Christian doctrines could be readily grasped. Lucas's sermons accomplish the same goals. Three Scripture readings are provided for each sermon: an Old Testament lesson, an Epistle, and a Gospel. Then the appropriate section of the *Catechism* along with Luther's explanation is given. Since 22 sermons are on the Creed for nearly half the church year, explanations for the three parts are read over several Sundays. Congregations will be very familiar with this section of the *Catechism*. Included with each sermon is a prayer, which in most cases is slightly longer than the length of the traditional collects. Twelve sermons, one for each month, are accompanied by an object lesson which is no longer than a brief paragraph in length.

The major focus for Luther in the *Small Catechism* were the Ten Commandments, the Apostles' Creed, and the Lord's Prayer. These comprised the core of his devotional life and were to be recited by the people several times a day. Appropriately, 45 of the sermons cover these areas. The remaining seven sermons are on Baptism, the Office of the Keys and Confession, and the Sacrament of the Altar. Luther used the First Commandment in his *Large Catechism* for his magnificent explanation of faith as trust in God and not for a diatribe against the wooden idols of the pagans. Lucas exhibits similar evangelical freedom in using the sermon on this commandment to give a forthright confession on the deity of Jesus and then moving right into the topic of the Trinity. Readers and listeners do not have to wait for the sermons on the second article of the Creed to hear about the person and work of Jesus. Sermons on the Second and Third Commandments are also deliberately christological in showing that Jesus is the object of faith and worship. The remaining seven commandments, the ones dealing with human social relations, also present Jesus as the preacher and the model of faith. Preaching on the Sixth Commandment is often a sensitive business. By counting the words that Saint Paul uses to speak about sexual relations, Lucas shows that the greater responsibility in this area is on the man. In the sermons on the Commandments, the writer's purpose is not to retell the Old Testament stories, but to direct the word of God immediately into the lives of Christians. In going through the Creed, Lucas can give a sermon on one word, "Lord," or he can give cogent discussions on the virgin birth and the resurrection. In his sermons on the Lord's Prayer, Lucas weaves Christ's life into the petitions. For example, in the petition on forgiving trespasses, Lucas presents Christ who forgave his enemies. Clearly the author has a profoundly developed exegetical skill, but avoids the minutia, the inclusion of which often ruins a sermon for those unversed in technical jargon. Sermons on the Sacraments bring this series to a convincing conclusion. Having followed Christ through the first sermons, the hearer is ready to join his Redeemer in Baptism, Absolution, and the Lord's Supper.

 Each sermon can be delivered in less than ten minutes, depending on the rate of speaking. Each sermon is tightly packed. No words are wasted. But if Lucas's brevity attracts, then so does his direct and forthright style. Readers never find themselves asking what is the point. Someone who is still uncomfortable with object lessons will find Lucas's suggestions in his children's sermons ready to use.

 Each person will have to determine the best use of these sermons. Pastors who have a midweek service and want to give their people a different fare than what is served on Sunday will find an immediate treasure here. These services, even with Communion, can be kept within thirty minutes. A Lucas sermon will deliver the Gospel completely and succinctly and keep the attention of the congregation. Since his language is always down-to-earth, the sermons are easily adapted for Lutheran elementary and high schools. Some will want to use them for private devotions. Laypeople, serving in remote places and foreign countries without access to their church, will greatly benefit from these sermons for conducting small group worship. The first great appeal is that all this comes in between two covers. Equally attractive is that these sermons present the Lutheran heritage in the language of the ordinary man. How Luther-like!

David P. Scaer

Author's Preface

Our age is one, we are told, in which there is no time for devotion. Certainly it is harder today than it used to be to gather Christians together for instruction in the truths of their faith. One of the most valuable and time-tested aids to personal and corporate devotion possessed by the church, the *Small Catechism* of Dr. Martin Luther, lends itself well in a variety of circumstances to the instruction of both young people and adults in cultivating life with God.

This book grew out of an idea I had to put a booklet of sermons on the catechism into the hands of the members of my first parish in Wauneta and Palisade, Nebraska. My prayer was that the sermons would help God's people see the catechism as more than a set of doctrines. Rather, I hoped to show how the catechism can point us to Christ.

These sermons can be used for personal devotions. They can also be used as youth group openings, as nursing home services, as studies for small group nurture and discussion, and as sermons from the pulpit. Those sermons which have an object lesson to go with them were ones I preached on the second Sunday of the month, which explains why some of these meditations have object lessons and others don't. Since I couldn't be involved with Sunday school, I brought Sunday school into the pulpit.

Included also are Scripture lessons for each Sunday which are keyed to the meaning of the catechism selection of the day, and also hymns chosen to focus upon the ideas presented in each sermon. In every case, the Scripture lesson given in bold type serves as the text for the sermon it accompanies.

May you find new riches in the Word of God through these sermons on Luther's *Small Catechism*, as God's Spirit grants grace.

James A. Lucas
September 14, 1999

Deuteronomy 11:26-32
Colossians 1:15-20
John 10:31-38

1. The First Commandment: Eyes On Jesus

> **THE FIRST COMMANDMENT**
> Thou shalt have no other gods before Me. *What does this mean?* We should fear, love, and trust in God above all things.

Art Linkletter saw a small boy drawing a picture. He inquired, "What are you drawing?" The small boy replied, "A picture of God." Linkletter told the lad that no one knows what God looks like, to which the boy confidently responded, "They will when I get through." Lots of people are running around today telling us that they have the inside scoop about who God is. Some come knocking on doors. Others pass out stuff at airports and train stations. Others peddle their secrets on late night television. And what about right around us? How many churches are scattered around the area all claiming to teach the truth about God?

We have an idea about who God really is. A Jewish rabbi named Jesus of Nazareth went around claiming that He was God. I know of two occasions when religious leaders in Jesus' day were ready to stone Jesus to death because of His claims. They finally succeeded in convicting Jesus of blasphemy and executing Him. The Jewish leaders had logic and common sense on their side. "How can the infinite God fit in a measly little speck of dust such as a man? How can Jesus be God?" That's like believing that we could stuff the earth into a thimble. It seems impossible to believe that God could fit into Jesus. Yet this is what we believe!

Many people think that we are silly for believing such a thing. Some say Jesus was a great moral teacher. Others say He was an inspired leader. Some, like the Moslems, believe Jesus was a great prophet, on the same level as Moses or Elijah or Isaiah. But few people are willing to believe that Jesus could be God. Many are willing to say Jesus was a good and holy man, even a prophet maybe, but not God. But hear what one former unbeliever has to say about the idea that Jesus could be a moral teacher and claim to be God. "A man who was merely a man and said the sort of things Jesus said wouldn't be a great moral teacher. He'd either be a lunatic — on the level with a man who says he's a poached egg — or else he'd be the devil of hell. You must make your choice. Either this man was, and is, the Son of God, or else a madman or something worse" (C. S. Lewis, *Mere Christianity*, New York: The Macmillan Co., 1952, 40). A man who claims to be God must either be a nut or demon-possessed. If Jesus is not God, then He is an idolater — He told people He was God. That would break the First Commandment, if Jesus weren't God.

The Apostle Paul made a clear confession about Jesus: "He is the image of the invisible God," "by him all things were created," "He is before all things, and in Him all things hold together," "for God was pleased to have all his fullness dwell in Him, and through Him to reconcile to Himself all things." Now, either Paul was a fool, like David Koresh's followers down there in Waco, Texas, who were willing to be burned to death with him believing his claims to be Jesus Christ, or a fake, someone who thought he could make a fast buck selling this religion to gullible Christians, or Paul's faith was true.

We can strain our brain trying to understand how God can be Father, Son, and Holy Spirit and not get very far. But we can get to know Jesus Christ and get a good idea from him who God really is. From Jesus we learn that God wants to save us from this evil and damaged world. From Jesus we learn that God's plan uses evil as a tool to bless His people, thereby showing His power over evil. While it would be a display of divine power to stop evil in its tracks, how much greater is the power that lets evil run its course and then makes evil turn into good at the end, better than things were before evil came along! Jesus showed that in His own life and death and resurrection.

How can Jesus be God? How can a mere man be God? A man was shown a glass bottle and asked what he thought was in the bottle. He replied in succession, "Well, it looks like wine or brandy or whiskey." When told it was full of white milk, he could not believe it until he saw the milk poured out. What he hadn't known, of course, was that the bottle was made of red glass, and its redness hid the color of the milk it contained. So it was and is with the Lord's humanity. People saw Him tired, hungry, suffering, weeping, and thought He was only man. He was made in the likeness of men, yet He ever is God over all, blessed forever. "For God was pleased to have all his fullness dwell in Him." The human body of Jesus was the bottle into which God poured himself. How God did it, I leave to him. It's no fun watching a magic show if I have to know how every trick is done. In a greater way, what good would it do me if God explained how He performs any miracle, let alone the grand miracle of pouring himself into human flesh! Instead, we sit back and enjoy the grand miracle of God pouring himself into Jesus.

All I know is that the Jesus who is in the Bible is the only God ever to give me the idea that God is gracious and able to save me completely from all evil. Jesus Christ is the only God who turns the kind of bad things that happen to people into blessings. Jesus showed complete mastery over the forces of nature. He showed authority over the enemies of humankind, the kind of authority a victorious general shows over the troops and people of the defeated country. He alone has undone death. No one stood outside His grave and told Him to come out. He raised Himself from death! If a dead man can tell himself to come back to life — that's significant! If Jesus isn't God, then we are without hope. All we would have left is the other gods of this world who expect us to earn a place in heaven, or worse, the gods who would condemn us to endless cycles of lives. Who is God? Let us join with saints of all time and all places who have pointed to the crucified and risen Lord Jesus.

Prayer: Holy Spirit, whose mission is to help us believe in Jesus, once again we ask that You would blow away all the smoke and dust that confuses us about who God really is. Keep our eyes fixed on Jesus Christ so that we may confess Him as our Lord and God. Help us to get to know the Father in heaven by helping us to get to know Jesus. Bless our study of the Bible so that we may always get to know Jesus better than before. Forgive our doubts and strengthen our faith. For Jesus' sake we pray. Amen.

Isaiah 9:1-7
Ephesians 5:15-20
John 16:17-28

2. The Second Commandment: God's Name

> **THE SECOND COMMANDMENT**
> Thou shalt not take the name of the Lord, thy God, in vain. *What does this mean?* We should fear and love God that we may not curse, swear, use witchcraft, lie, or deceive by His name, but call upon it in every trouble, pray, praise, and give thanks.

The Second Commandment warns us against using God's name in an empty and improper manner. Anyone who is a parent can understand this. How many times do children call or yell out, "Mom!" or "Dad!" and then ask for something trivial, or worse, something you don't want them to have (the whining in grocery and discount stores over candy and toys!). Children use their parents' names to interrupt, without regard for what the parents are doing. Children ask Dad when they don't get their way with Mom, abusing her name. Parents have been called upon to do things they don't like being asked. I suppose parents' names are abused more than any other person — except maybe God's name.

In God's name, people have cursed all manner of people, animals, and objects. Hell would truly be crowded if God damned all the things and people he has been asked to damn. In God's name, people have lied in courtrooms. Christians lie in God's name when they tell any lie because people look at us and expect Christians to tell the truth. Many people call upon God through horoscopes and other witchcraft. God says, "Call upon me in the day of trouble and I will answer you." But many people, including some Christians, look to horoscopes, ouija boards, tea leaves, fortune tellers, and such for answers to their prayers. That's praying to God, through the devil, instead of through Christ! Every religion or denomination or preacher that doesn't teach the truth as handed down from the apostles has used God's name in vain. It is an abuse of God's name to teach false doctrine. But the worst abuse of God's name is when people do not call upon Jesus Christ for forgiveness of sins and eternal life.

Consider what Jesus said: "I tell you the truth, my Father will give you whatever you ask in my name. Until now you have not asked for anything in my name. Ask and you will receive, and your joy will be complete." But which Jesus should we call on? I believe Jesus gives us the answer when He said, "The Father himself loves you because you have loved me and have believed that I came from God. I came from the Father and entered the world; now I am leaving the world and going back to the Father." Prophets came from God, but only Jesus comes from God from outside of creation and enters into it. Any Jesus who did not exist before the world and who is not sitting with the Father ruling all creation is a false Jesus.

Saint Paul teaches us that "Therefore God exalted [Jesus] to the highest place and gave him the name that is above every name, that at the name of Jesus every knee should bow, in heaven and on earth and under the earth, and every tongue confess that Jesus Christ is Lord, to the glory of God the Father." What is the name above all names? God. Jesus has that name. In addition, Jesus is called Lord. "Lord" is the word used in the Bible of Jesus' day for the name of God, just as today when people say that they believe in the Lord. Very clearly, Paul wants us to believe that Jesus is the Lord God's people prayed to in the Old Testament.

The kinds of prayers God answers are those prayed through the Jesus who humbled himself until He died in our place, but who also rose from the dead and lives and is king forever. Jesus Christ is the lens that focuses our prayers on the heart of God. When our prayers go through Jesus, like a filter lens, he strips them of sin. Then, like a lens, Jesus amplifies our true need. In fact, after our prayers go through Jesus, they may not even sound like the prayers we thought we prayed. After sin is filtered out and the true need the

Spirit found in our soul is magnified, a prayer offered according to God's will is offered to Him. The answer we get will be at least what we ask for, but more often, better. So if you don't get what you ask for, expect something better! Lots of people pray to someone called God, but only those prayers prayed in Jesus' name get heard by the God who created heaven and earth. We don't have to end our prayers with the words, "In the name of Jesus," for our prayers to be in His name. To pray in the name of Jesus is to pray with His authority. Those who have been baptized and believe in Jesus have the right to use His name, His authority to pray, according to his own promise, "I tell you the truth, my Father will give you whatever you ask in my name ... because you have loved me and have believed that I came from God."

Prayer: Holy Spirit, help us believe more than ever before in Jesus Christ as the Lord to whom we may pray, and through whom we may pray to God the Father. Teach us to pray in His name and to honor His name with all we say and do in this life. Amen.

Object lesson: Object in bag: Play money. Tell the children that you have a sack full of money. Then show them the money. Talk about how "real" the money is. Tell them that money which is fake is called counterfeit. Tell them how bankers can tell counterfeit money just by the feel (because they can be fooled by how it looks).

Talk about fake Jesuses. Ask them if a fake Jesus could do the things the real Jesus did. Ask them to tell some of the things the real Jesus did (die on the cross, rise again, sit at right hand of the Father, answer our prayers). Point out that this is the test to find fake Jesuses. Fake Jesuses aren't really the God we can pray to for salvation. Point out that they can learn about the real Jesus if they go to Sunday school and church often and regularly. Tell them they can pray to Jesus.

Exodus 20:8-11
Acts 2:36-47
Matthew 11:25-30

3. The Third Commandment: Holding God's Word Sacred

> **THE THIRD COMMANDMENT**
> Remember the Sabbath day, to keep it holy. *What does this mean?* We should fear and love God that we may not despise preaching and His Word, but hold it sacred and gladly hear and learn it.

When is the Sabbath day? Most seem to agree that Sunday is the Sabbath day. What makes Sunday the Sabbath day? A story may help answer this. A church member who had previously been attending services regularly, suddenly stopped coming to church. After some weeks, the minister decided to visit the absent member. It was a chilly evening, and the minister found the man at home alone, sitting before a blazing fire. Guessing the reason for his pastor's visit, the man welcomed him, led him to a big chair by the fireplace, and waited. The minister made himself comfortable and said nothing. In grave silence, he contemplated the play of the flames around the burning logs. After some minutes, he took the fire tongs, carefully picked up a brightly burning ember and placed it to one side of the hearth. Then he sat back in his chair, still silent. The host watched all this in quiet fascination. As the lone ember's flame diminished, there was a momentary glow, but then its fire was no more and it was cold and dead. Not a word had been spoken since the initial greetings. But as the minister rose to leave, the host said, "Thank you so much for your visit — and especially for your fiery sermon. I shall be at church next Sunday."

What happens when Christians go to church? The pastor made the point that Christians who drop out of church end up like a coal taken out of a fire — cold and dead. But something great happens when Christians get together. Each adds energy to the others and great things happen. Consider the early church in the days shortly after Jesus rose from the dead. When people were told the good news about Jesus, Luke reports, "They devoted themselves to the apostles' teaching and to the fellowship, to the breaking of bread and to prayer." To be devoted meant sacrificing the time it took to get to know better what the apostles taught about Jesus. As our catechism teaches, these people held preaching very sacred, and gladly heard and learned the Word of God as often as they could. They gathered regularly for Bible class and Holy Communion.

"All the believers were together and had everything in common. Selling their possessions and goods, they gave to anyone as he had need." Those first Christians invented welfare after they realized what Jesus had done for them. Salvation is something Christians do, as well as something we talk about. The good news that Jesus died and rose again to save us from sin, death, and the power of the devil also includes the good news that Jesus sends us to love the needy in His name.

"Every day they continued to meet together in the temple courts." That will blow your mind: they didn't meet only once a week. They had church every day. This custom was followed in many parts of the world up to this present day. We could have services every day. Our hymnal has services for each day of the week, at least twice a day. The Matins service is the morning service for each weekday. Vespers is the evening service. Luther had services twice a day during the week, and three times on Sundays. Christians still offer services every day in many places in the world. That's because every day is the Sabbath day now. Remember, Jesus said, "Come to me, all you who labor and are heavy laden, and I will give you rest." The Sabbath day was a day of rest for God's people that taught them what Jesus would do when He came. The Sabbath day pointed to Jesus, like everything else God's people did in the Old Testament days. Now, any day we go to Jesus is a Sabbath day, not just Sunday.

"They broke bread in their homes and ate together with glad and sincere hearts, praising God and enjoying the favor of all the people." Early Christians looked to each other for social fulfillment. They didn't need a VFW hall or school activities to get together. They believed that they were the body of Jesus and acted that out. They spent a lot of time in each others' homes. Remember, there were no churches where they could meet in those days. Such a thing didn't come along for over three hundred years! Pastors traveled from home to home. But many services were held without pastors. We have potluck dinners once in a while. In those days, every day, somewhere, Christians were meeting for potluck dinners.

"And the Lord added to their number daily those who were being saved." That's what happens when Christians take Jesus seriously. The secret to a growing congregation is that the members of that congregation are devoted to God's Word and to each other. It's not the pastor who makes a church grow. It's not members being friendly before or after church services that makes a church grow. It's not attractive programs that make a church grow. These have influence, but they are not the secret. Plain and simple, what makes a church grow is plenty of Bible study and plenty of time spent with each other. An hour or so a week in church, maybe, if you feel like it, hardly counts for the kind of devotion growing churches will have.

The Scripture lays a challenge before us: remember Jesus! We are challenged to make Jesus Christ a big part of our life. Think how tired we are because we don't spend more time with Jesus and those He has saved! Think how this congregation would blossom if we would take Jesus at his Word and spend more time with Him and each other!

Prayer: Holy Spirit, You come from Jesus to give us faith and life. Forgive us for taking Jesus for granted and crowding Him out of our lives with all the cares of this world. Help us to believe that we don't have to spend so much time making a living that we only have a few minutes a week to spend with You and each other. Help us believe that we will find more joy and fulfillment when we soak ourselves in Your Word and share our lives with each other. Amen.

Proverbs 23:22-25
Ephesians 6:1-9
Mark 7:5-15

4. The Fourth Commandment: Holding Parents In Love And Esteem

> THE FOURTH COMMANDMENT
> Thou shalt honor thy father and thy mother, that it may be well with thee, and thou mayest live long on the earth. *What does this mean?* We should fear and love God that we may not despise our parents and masters, nor provoke them to anger, but give them honor, serve and obey them, and hold them in love and esteem.

Many people are called "father" in the Bible. In addition to God and dads, prophets, priests, and kings are also called fathers. Even Jesus is called Father! Israel is called a mother. God is like a mother. Jesus wanted to gather the Israelites as a hen gathers chicks. So, when God says we are to honor father and mother, He is speaking of more than the people we call Mom and Dad. A father is one who sustains life. A mother is one who gives life. Fathers and mothers reflect God's care for us.

So, what right do we have to be disrespectful to them? You know what I mean. We ignore Mom and Dad when we don't agree with them. We have been sassy and mouthy to our moms and dads, and disobeyed them. And how many times have we also sinned against others who are fathers and mothers to us? We poke fun at presidents and congressmen and other politicians, or say bad things about them. We ignore laws that we don't agree with or outright defy them, as when people buy radar detectors or when they cheat on their tax reporting. We grumble about our bosses and do poor work when we feel angry about them. We talk negatively about the pastor and resist his leadership when we don't agree with him. We give teachers a bad time by lack of self-control in classrooms.

Our Lord Jesus looks down on our disrespect of those who are fathers and mothers to us. He said to people in his day, "You have a fine way of setting aside the commands of God in order to observe your own traditions! For Moses said, 'Honor your father and your mother,' and, 'Anyone who curses his father or mother must be put to death.' But you say that if a man says to his father or mother: 'Whatever help you might otherwise have received from me is Corban' (that is, a gift devoted to God), then you no longer let him do anything for his father or mother. Thus you nullify the word of God by your tradition that you have handed down." Those guys had taken money they should have spent to take care of their parents and given it to the church instead, thinking they were doing something better. Today, we do the same thing when we do what we think is right instead of being obedient and respectful to those in authority over us.

No matter how much we may disagree with those God has put in authority over us, we must remember that they are a reflection of His care. If we think we have a right to show disrespect to those God has put over us, we are showing dishonor to Jesus Christ, who is Father over them all. He is the Master of masters. He is the King of kings. He is the Teacher of teachers and preachers. It is Jesus who put a president in the White House and who appointed all the politicians of the world besides. It is Jesus who calls men and women to teach children and to run our schools. It is Jesus who put all those pastors in all those churches. It is Jesus who gave us our jobs. If we think any other way, we forget who is Father and Mother of all fathers and mothers.

True, at times, the reflection we see of God in earthly fathers and mothers may be warped or badly flawed. We may shake our heads in disgust about some of the parents God has given us because these parents don't match the high standards God has set for them. But no matter how badly earthly fathers and mothers behave, one thing remains true — they are still our mothers and fathers. And because of that, no matter how bad mothers and fathers and government leaders and pastors and teachers and bosses and employers may be, God blesses us through them.

Governments, no matter how humanistic or wicked, do keep basic law and order in this world. Employers and bosses, no matter how cheap or unfair they may be, do put bread and butter on our tables. Teachers, no matter how incompetent or anti-family they may be, do teach some basic skills we can use to get along in this world. And pastors, no matter how stupid, lazy, or confused they may be on every point of doctrine, do lead us to Jesus when they baptize us and pronounce forgiveness of sins to us. Furthermore, the more we respect those in authority, the more they can bless us. Didn't God promise that if we honored them, "it may be well with [us] and [we] may live long on the earth?"

Jesus told the parent-neglecting Pharisees and rabbis of His day that what comes out of a man makes him unclean. We have been cleansed on the inside by the renewing power of Jesus' Spirit. Why should we allow disrespect for authority to defile us and make us like everyone else? With the Spirit's help, we can show proper respect for authority and thereby enjoy the blessing of prosperity that comes with doing that.

Prayer: Holy Father in heaven, for Jesus' sake, make us into children who always show respect and honor to those in authority. Forgive us our disobedience and disrespect. As You have cleansed our hearts by the blood of Jesus, cleanse our lives that in all things we may honor You, Father over all. Amen.

Proverbs 31:1-7
Romans 12:9-21
Matthew 25:31-47

5. The Fifth Commandment: Help And Befriend

> **THE FIFTH COMMANDMENT**
> Thou shalt not kill. *What does this mean?* We should fear and love God that we may not hurt nor harm our neighbor in his body, but help and befriend him in every bodily need.

If anyone deserves to be killed, it's me. "The wages of sin is death." I have sinned in more ways than I care to remember (and members of my family and others can fill you in on sins I have forgotten). Yet, I celebrate life with you today — you, who also deserve to be killed for your many sins. While some murderous human might walk up to me one day and take my life, I don't have to fear that God will. In fact, because Jesus died for our sins, we are confident that we can't really die. A murderer, or even an executioner, or a car wreck, or disease, or old age or something else may take our life, but God will give it back to us.

God clothed Himself in flesh and blood in Jesus Christ so that we could be His neighbor. Jesus once defined a neighbor as anyone who is in need. We are neighbors to Jesus. Jesus is our Good Samaritan. And because of that, we know that God will not hurt nor harm us in our bodies, but will help and befriend us in every bodily need. The food we eat, the clothes we wear, the jobs we hold, the homes we live in — all are testimonies of the life-giving plans Jesus Christ has for us forgiven sinners.

However, remember that all that we have to support our life comes to us from God through others around us. I don't grow the food I eat. I don't mine the minerals or harvest the trees that make up so much of what I own. I do not have my job by my own willpower. All that I have either comes directly from God, like the air I breathe or the sun that keeps me warm, or comes to me from what people like you do in Christ's name. We take care of each other as agents of life representing the Prince of life, Jesus Christ.

Consider a few remarks made by the Apostle Paul how we can be agents of life in a dying world. "Be devoted to one another in brotherly love. Honor one another above yourselves." Jesus did this for us when He laid down His life for us — total dedication. He humbled Himself so we could be lifted up. He made Himself to be poor so we could become rich. So how can we dedicate ourselves to each other in like manner? First, Paul directs, "Share with God's people who are in need." Christians invented welfare as a way of imitating the generosity of Jesus to us. Let's take it back from the government, and especially look out for those who belong to our church. Many of the church-related fraternal organizations are a start. What about looking out for members who need time, as well as money, to get by? Paul also adds, "Practice hospitality." Jesus has invited us to live and eat with him forever. Why not do the same with each other? Why not open up our homes to each other and those we want to include in the household of faith?

What about those people we don't like, or who hurt us? "Bless those who persecute you; bless and do not curse." Forgiveness is the hand that feeds the mouth that bites you. Parents do it with children. Children often bite the hand that feeds them — by disobedience, hateful remarks, and other acts of rebellion. Yet parents continue to care for their children, hoping that the love they show their children will help a relationship of respect and love to grow from child to parent. Christ does it for us.

"Rejoice with those who rejoice." All good things come from Jesus, even if more comes to you than to me. Forgiveness means being happy when our enemy prospers, remembering that God shows the same mercy to us.

"Mourn with those who mourn." When one of us is a victim of the robbers and killers running loose in the world, the rest of us can join with Jesus in comforting. "Do not repay anyone evil for evil. Be careful to do what is right in the eyes of everybody. If it is possible, as far as it depends on you, live at peace with everyone." Two wrongs don't make a right. The murder of a doctor who commits murder on unborn children is still murder. We can do more for the victims of evil in this world if we forgive and show mercy on the victimizers, just as Jesus showed mercy on those who murdered him.

"Do not take revenge, my friends, but leave room for God's wrath, for it is written: 'It is mine to avenge; I will repay,' says the Lord." Jesus did not tell us to get rid of evil. That's His job. He can do a better job of it, anyway. Remember that Jesus keeps track of the bad that happens to you. He will make it right. And woe to them on whom His vengeance falls for our sake!

"On the contrary: 'If your enemy is hungry, feed him; if he is thirsty, give him something to drink. In doing this, you will heap burning coals on his head.' Do not be overcome by evil, but overcome evil with good." Those last words remind us how Jesus deals with evil. The devil uses force to get things changed. Jesus uses goodness. The plan Jesus has for changing the world includes preaching and teaching the good news about the death and resurrection Jesus did for us. The good news we proclaim is amplified when we help and befriend our neighbors. By our kindness to enemies we can do what Jesus does for us.

Prayer: Holy Spirit, help us to be merciful in all that we do. Help us to bring life and happiness to those around us. Forgive us the many times we have made people unhappy or miserable with the anger and hate that is in us. Take that anger and hate away so that we may show kindness, forgiveness, and mercy to all, especially our enemies. Amen.

Object lesson: What's the best way to get rid of an enemy? A gun? No, it's against the law to kill someone. Tie him up? No, it's wrong to hold someone against his will. How about what President Abraham Lincoln did? In the few days between the end of the Civil War and his death, President Lincoln allowed a group of former rebels into his office for a visit. They complained about their harsh treatment. But President Lincoln's gentle, friendly manner soon thawed the ice, and the Southerners left with a new respect for their old enemy. A Northern congressman approached the president and criticized him for "befriending the enemy," suggesting that instead of befriending them he should have had them shot for the traitors they were. Lincoln smiled and replied, "Am I not destroying my enemies by making them my friends?"

The best way to get rid of an enemy is to forgive him so he can become a friend. This is what Jesus did when He forgave us our sins. We show we forgive by doing good things for our enemies. Think how Jesus shows us that He forgives us. Jesus took our sins to His cross. He won the war against the devil for us. He is getting a place in heaven ready for us. What good things can we do to show our enemies we forgive them? How about being polite and kind? Or giving them food and clothing if they need them? Or showing friendliness to them, even when they are not friendly to you?

Genesis 2:15-25
Ephesians 5:21-33
Mark 10:1-12

6. The Sixth Commandment: A Chaste And Decent Life

> THE SIXTH COMMANDMENT
> Thou shalt not commit adultery. *What does this mean?*
> We should fear and love God that we may lead a chaste and decent life in word and deed, and each love and honor his spouse.

You don't have to be married to commit adultery. Adultery happens whenever we use sexual intimacy to trash another person's life or our own. The Bible talks about lust (desiring a sexual relationship with someone forbidden to you), fornication (sexual relationship outside of marriage, to treat a woman as a whore — sex without commitment — such as premarital sex), homosexuality (sexual relationship with someone of the same gender) — all these are the same as adultery.

Today, we could add pornography as a form of adultery — both "soft core" (like what you find in a lot of women's magazines, on soap operas, and other R-rated entertainment), and "hard core" (like what is found in X-rated movies and dirty magazines). Pornography has one goal — sexual perversion: to hook into lust and encourage fornication, homosexuality, and adultery.

The most visible victim of adultery is marriage, the most intimate relationship. It is so intimate that the Apostle Paul teaches in his letter to the Ephesians that the sexual relationship of a good marriage is the closest thing to what salvation is all about. We are married to Jesus. That affects sexuality.

"Wives, submit to your husbands as to the Lord. For the husband is the head of the wife as Christ is the head of the church, his body, of which he is the Savior. Now as the church submits to Christ, so also wives should submit to their husbands in everything." I can imagine that many women cringe with disgust when they hear that word "submit." Wives have always submitted to their husbands; in many cases they have been forced to submit. For many women, these words make them think of slavery, being a doormat, or something else unpleasant.

However, in the Bible, the word "submit" has the same meaning as a yield sign. Jesus puts up yield signs in our lives. A yield sign keeps us safe when many of us want to use the same intersection at the same time. When we submit to each other, we are yielding the right of way to the other person. It doesn't make you less of a person to submit any more than yielding at an intersection would make me less of a person. In fact, if I don't yield when I should, that's when I become less of a person. A woman yielding to a man the way God wants her to, is doing the safe thing. So here is a message about safe sex.

Safe sex for women includes when a woman yields to her man as though he were Jesus, her Savior. Is this what feminism teaches? Is this what soap operas teach? Is this what you read in those women's magazines? Doesn't the world teach that if a woman yields to a man she is foolish? Women are taught to take charge of themselves. Women are taught that their sexuality is at risk because men are like hungry wolves looking for tasty sheep to enjoy. Unmarried women are taught that they must manage men's sex drives so that women can get what they want without giving the men what they want. Married women are taught that they are in sexual bondage.

But, what does the church lose by yielding to Jesus? What does the church lose by being the partner who yields to the will of Jesus? Only sin and death! Women who yield to their men as though those men were Jesus will be safe from committing sexual sins.

The Apostle Paul has instructions for men how to have safe sex with their women. Paul had 58 words to say to women. However, he had 153 words for the men. That means men have greater responsibility. "Husbands, love your wives, just as Christ loved the church and gave himself up for her to make her holy, cleansing her by the washing with water through the word, and to present her to himself as a radiant church, without stain or wrinkle or any other blemish, but holy and blameless." That describes safe sex! Sex outside marriage stains and wrinkles women no matter what anyone tells you.

Jesus died to take away the sin of people like you and me. He died so we, His church, His bride, could be pure, free from shame. Men should be willing to die so that their women can be free from shame and guilt. Why not then also be willing to live for them? Wait until women can safely have sex in marriage, and then treat the women's sexuality as Christ treats the church? Men, why not cleanse from your life anything that cheapens sex — girlie pictures, dirty jokes? Why not avoid those situations that inflame male lust — television programs, videos, movies that glamorize sex or nudity? Why not stand up for women who are being commercially exploited by the fashion, pornography, and abortion industries?

"In this same way, husbands ought to love their wives as their own bodies. He who loves his wife loves himself. After all, no one ever hated his own body, but he feeds and cares for it, just as Christ does the church — for we are members of his body." A wedding license is not a hunting license. A man promises to cherish his wife and care for her. Jesus offers forgiveness of sins to us when we sin. Forgiveness is a fundamental ingredient of marriage. The vows married people make are usually broken very soon. What keeps a couple together is the same thing that keeps Christ and his church together. And it seems clear to me that men should be the first to forgive and be forgiving.

"For this reason a man will leave his father and mother and be united to his wife, and the two will become one flesh. This is a profound mystery — but I am talking about Christ and the church. However, each one of you also must love his wife as he loves himself, and the wife must respect her husband." A sexual union must be based on mutual trust. A man can't keep his options open. A man burns his bridges behind him when he takes a woman. Jesus married us. He holds nothing back. Jesus knows nothing of prenuptial agreements — how things will be divided up at divorce. Men should be willing to do that for their women.

But all this is under one verse: "Submit to one another out of reverence for Christ." The very first thing Paul said was that children and parents, or employers and employees, as well as men and women, should yield to each other. We can do that because Jesus yielded His rights to see to it that we got what we needed.

Prayer: Holy Spirit, cleanse our hearts of all impurity of thought, word, and deed. Not one of us is too young or old to be affected by the sexual perversions that pollute our society. Forgive us of the sexual sins we have committed — any lust, any divorces, any premarital sex, any use of pornography and marriage unfaithfulness — forgive us of these sins as You forgive us of any sins: for the sake of the suffering and death of Jesus. Help our boys to grow up to be men who will respect and care for women as Christ does the church. Help our girls to grow up to be women who will respect and trust their men as You help the church to trust Jesus. Help the men and women of this church to live and work together in purity and harmony. Bless those who are married with extra faithfulness to each other. Bless those who are single with extra self-control. Help us to turn our backs to those who try to peddle sexual perversion to us. Help us to live clean and decent lives in a dirty world. Amen.

Genesis 14:14-16
2 Corinthians 8:1-9
Luke 12:22-34

7. The Seventh Commandment: Improve And Protect

> **THE SEVENTH COMMANDMENT**
> Thou shalt not steal. *What does this mean?* We should fear and love God that we may not take our neighbor's money or goods, nor get them by false ware or dealing, but help him to improve and protect his property and business.

How much do you really fear and love God? Are you willing to let someone else have more than you have and be glad about it? Or do you complain because you aren't paid as much as other people you know who seem to do less work or hold less responsibility than you do? Are you willing to dip into your own pockets to take food off your own table and clothes off your own back to help out someone who is down and out? Or do you read about pleas for money to help flood or famine victims and think, "Too bad for them, but I have my own problems?" The Bible teaches us that a thief is more than someone who robs or tricks you out of property. A thief is also someone who hoards goods for himself for fear that he won't have enough if he shares with others. A thief is someone who stands by and does nothing while he sees the property and business of someone else go down the drain. A person who neglects to help a needy person for fear of being short on goods himself, is as much a thief as the person who robs banks, cheats, or steals.

Jesus tells us why we don't have to be thieves. "Do not worry ... For the pagan world runs after all such things, and your Father knows that you need them. Do not be afraid, little flock, for your Father has been pleased to give you the kingdom." We are free to be generous (the opposite of being a thief) because we have a Father who knows what we need and who has promised to make us kings. The death of Jesus on the cross and the way He came back to life again shows that God is not going to let us be ruined by the worst that can happen to us. We no longer have to be afraid of the devil robbing us of our lives. God will pay us back! How much less do we need to fear being short on earthly goods? Rich people are not secure because they have so much. Instead, they surround themselves with alarms and guards. They are afraid of losing something! Fear lies at the root of stealing. A thief steals because he is afraid he won't be able to get good things any other way. But we have a Father in heaven who gives all good things, who especially looks out for those who belong to Jesus Christ.

The story has been told of a man who was caught and taken to court because he had stolen a loaf of bread. When the judge investigated, he found out that the man had no job, and his family was hungry. He had tried unsuccessfully to get work and finally, to feed his family, he had stolen a loaf of bread. Although recognizing the extenuating circumstances, the judge said, "I'm sorry, but the law can make no exceptions. You stole, and therefore I have to punish you. I order you to pay a fine of ten dollars." He then continued, "But I want to pay the fine myself." He reached into his pocket, pulled out a ten-dollar bill, and handed it to the man.

As soon as the man took the money, the judge said, "Now I also want to forgive the fine. Furthermore, I am going to instruct the bailiff to pass around a hat to everyone in this courtroom, and I am fining everyone in this courtroom fifty cents for living in a city where a man has to steal in order to have bread to eat." The money was collected and given to the defendant. This story illustrates what Jesus has done for us. He is the judge who forgives the thief and looks out for the poor. "I'll take care of you," He says.

How does He do that? What do you think of what Jesus said? "Sell your possessions and give to the poor. Provide purses for yourselves that will not wear out, a treasure in heaven that will not be exhausted, where no thief comes near and no moth destroys. For where your treasure is, there your heart will be also." Do we have to wait for Jesus to shame us as He passes the hat around? Or can we anticipate the needs of others and in a spirit of generosity (that filled Jesus, who owns the cattle on a thousand hills, to become poor so we could become rich) — can we anticipate those needs and cheerfully give towards them?

"God loves a cheerful giver." God doesn't need our money. He wants us. "Where our treasure is, their our hearts are also." Saint Paul writes about a church whose members were living in poverty, who took up a collection, taking food off their tables, in order to help Christians who lived nearly a thousand miles away — "all because they first gave themselves to the Lord." Their treasure was in heaven.

Will you be like General Sam Houston, who when he was baptized in a river refused to take his wallet out of his pocket? He told the preacher that his wallet got baptized too so that it also would belong to God. Will you be like the child who climbed into the collection plate when it was passed to her? Abraham risked his own life and the lives of 318 of his men to rescue his nephew Lot and his nephew's possessions. Lot made a bad business choice that cost him his goods. Yet Abraham rescued Lot and his possessions. We already hold title to a kingdom. What harm can come to us if for a few weeks or years we don't live like kings here? We can be generous, because we have a generous heavenly Father! He is going to take care of us, even if it doesn't seem like He gives us what we think we should get.

Prayer: Heavenly Father, help us believe that You will take much better care of us than You already do of birds like sparrows and weeds like lilies of the field. When we are well off, help us to be willing to share of our plenty with those in need. When times are tough, help us to be satisfied. Forgive us of envy we have towards those who are better off than we are. Forgive us when we fearfully collect goods. Give us the Spirit of Jesus that we may even sell all we have if in so doing we may help someone see Your sacrificial love and be drawn to Jesus. Amen.

Proverbs 31:8-9
James 4:1-12
Matthew 18:15-20

8. The Eighth Commandment: Speak Well Of Your Neighbor

> **THE EIGHTH COMMANDMENT**
> Thou shalt not bear false witness against thy neighbor.
> *What does this mean?* We should fear and love God that we may not deceitfully belie, betray, slander, nor defame our neighbor, but defend him, speak well of him, and put the best construction on everything.

What is a lie? In a courtroom we are asked to swear to tell the truth, the whole truth and nothing but the truth. Doesn't that mean that we should tell only what happens, and not leave out important details or add details that never happened? How many of you have ever testified in a court? Let me ask that again, only this time remember that a court is any place a person's character is on trial, whether or not the person is present — like down at the coffee shop, talking about someone who isn't there! Isn't gossip really testimony at a trial? The only difference between a gossip session and a trial is that the defendant isn't present to defend himself. Why do we like to report the bad things other people do? The difference between a gossip and a witness in a courtroom is like the difference between a butcher and a surgeon. Both cut the meat, but for different reasons.

It is natural that we like to tell stories about each other that make the other guy look bad. But anytime we do that, unless we are willing to face the other guy with our accusation, we are always lying. That's because gossip and slander, like any lie, don't allow the whole story to be told, namely the part of the story known by the person we gossip about. You may think you know the whole story, but until you have his testimony and those who could speak in his defense, you do not have the whole truth. And a half truth is as bad as a lie. It doesn't take into account what Jesus has to say either.

The very first thing to remember about anyone is that Jesus forgave any sins everyone commits. Along with this is the idea that Jesus thinks of us as royalty. So, what business do we have calling Jesus a liar? That's what we are doing when we gossip and backbite. Jesus forgives your sins. He also forgives mine — even if I am not around to defend myself.

But what are we supposed to do, then, when we think someone has treated us badly? Just let it go? Ignore it? No, that would not allow justice to work. The Lord Jesus tells us how to handle conflict so that forgiveness can have a chance to work healing between us. "If your brother sins against you, go and show him his fault, just between the two of you. If he listens to you, you have won your brother over." First, give the other guy a chance to repent. You might discover that what you thought the other guy did isn't really what happened, or what he intended. Jesus doesn't clobber us each time we sin. Instead He is willing to forgive us so we can go on being brothers.

"But if he will not listen, take one or two others along, 'so that every matter may be established by the testimony of two or three witnesses.'" If we can't get satisfaction, Jesus allows us to involve other people — but only so that certain facts can be established in case the matter has to go to public trial. But the goal is still to "settle out of court" if at all possible, and witnesses can be a big help to do this. The main fact we need to look for is, "Was a real attempt made to forgive and be forgiven?" Witnesses make sure a fair attempt was made to settle the matter in private.

"If he refuses to listen to them, tell it to the church." Jesus allows us to make public accusations only when all attempts at forgiveness have failed in private. Jesus sets up a church court. You all, when gathered in church, are the jury. Each side gets to tell its story, with the help of the witnesses. The whole congregation then sorts through the stories to try to find the truth. The church can help a person realize how serious his sin is so he can be forgiven.

If a person is found guilty of sin, and he still won't accept forgiveness, then — and only then — are we allowed to take action against him. But notice what action we are supposed to take: "and if he refuses to listen even to the church, treat him as you would a pagan or a tax collector." That means the unrepentant sinner becomes missionary material, and we start all over with him from the basics, teaching him about sin and grace.

Jesus gave this authority to the church with these words: "I tell you the truth, whatever you bind on earth will be bound in heaven, and whatever you loose on earth will be loosed in heaven. Again, I tell you that if two of you on earth agree about anything you ask for, it will be done for you by my Father in heaven. For where two or three come together in my name, there am I with them." We are allowed by Jesus to tell someone that his sins are forgiven, or that the forgiveness of his sins has been revoked until he repents. Our goal always is the same: forgive sins whenever possible, condemn sinners only when necessary. (The world thinks the opposite: Condemn sinners whenever possible; forgive sins only when necessary.)

The least we can do when we think someone is doing evil is give him the benefit of the doubt ("put the best construction on everything"). Sometimes what we see isn't the whole story. I have a photo of a friend of mine finishing a race. It is from my high school yearbook. It shows a runner crossing the finish line ahead of him. The caption under the photo names the runner in front as the winner. My friend got angry when he saw that! He said that he was the winner. Yet, there was the finish line stretched across the other runner's chest. My friend is obviously a step behind. However, a close look at the photo, near the very edge, shows that my friend has a baton in his hand. That means they were running a relay race. The other runner's hands are empty! That means the other runner had disqualified himself earlier by not taking the baton from his teammate. The yearbook editor looked at the obvious and jumped to the wrong conclusion! Appearances can be deceiving. "Putting the best construction on everything" means trying to figure out what good reason the other guy may have thought he had for doing what he did. It means believing that you might not know the whole story and trying to fill in the gaps with a defense.

Jesus died to take our sins to His grave. His death changed our past. That's the truth. Forgiveness heals our past. In a like manner, when we seek to forgive each other instead of tear each other down, we end up healing the breaks that damage our relationships to each other. It's always best to try to forgive. And if you think someone thinks you have done wrong to him, Jesus says, quick, go to him and be forgiven.

Prayer: Lord Jesus, You call us saints even though we sin daily. You treat us like royalty even though we often treat each other like dirt. You forgive us for crimes we commit against You even though we are eager to get even with those who sin against us. You speak well of us before the Father in heaven, even though we can hardly go a day without telling lies about each other. Help us tell the truth. Especially help us interpret what other people do in the best possible manner, giving them the benefit of the doubt until they show clearly in the presence of many witnesses that they are unwilling to do what is right. And even then, help us extend a forgiving hand, even if that hand is rejected. Amen.

Psalm 16:5-6
1 Timothy 6:6-10
Matthew 6:25-34

9. The Ninth Commandment: Help And Be Of Service

> **THE NINTH COMMANDMENT**
> Thou shalt not covet thy neighbor's house. *What does this mean?* We should fear and love God that we may not craftily seek to get our neighbor's inheritance or house, nor obtain it by a show of right, but help and be of service to him in keeping it.

In Psalm 16, David imagines Jesus Christ praying these words to God: "Jehovah is my choice portion and my cup; you securely hold my lot. The boundary lines have fallen for me in pleasant places; surely I have a delightful inheritance." Note how David uses real estate talk to show the kind of faith the perfect man has in Jehovah. In Bible times, real estate was passed down through each generation by laws God had set down. We have laws of humankind to do that today. We have these laws because everyone has a fundamental need for a place to live and make a livelihood. God wrote inheritance laws for His people. These laws showed how God wanted to provide a lasting home for His people. Since people don't last long, God taught the idea of "forever" by giving a farm to a family "forever." The property was divided among the children with the oldest son getting twice what everyone else got. A man could not sell his farm. He could only lease it, and then only until the next Jubilee year which came every fifty years. The family farm was a shadow cast by an eternal inheritance in heaven. Perfect faith looked past mere dirt and trees on earth to a home and estate in heaven.

Jesus Christ had that faith. Jesus had no place of His own in this world — "Foxes have holes and birds have nests, but the son of man does not have a place to lay his head." Jesus left no property behind because He had none to leave behind. He was dirt poor. Jesus relied on money, food, and shelter donated by those He taught. Yet Jesus was the richest man in the universe! He held title to heaven and earth. Even more, the Bible says that we are His inheritance. We are His most prized possession. When Jesus sang Psalm 16 in church, He was thinking about you and me and all those the Father had given Him.

When we sing Psalm 16, we also have an inheritance for which to thank God. We may not have a lot of real estate. But, didn't Jesus promise that He is preparing a place for us in His Father's house? Didn't He promise us treasure in heaven that can't be stolen or spoiled? Heaven is our inheritance. That's because we are really inheriting Jesus. He is the priceless treasure which the Father has left to us. On the night before Jesus died He sealed His last will and testament. A testament tells what one wants to happen after one dies. What happened after Jesus gave us the cup of the blood of His testament? He died. What did He leave us? In that testament He left us forgiveness of sins. What can a six-thousand-acre farm do for you that will last into eternity?

What joy can a nice house, a big yard, and tons of appliances really bring you? You only end up with more grass to mow, more walls to wash and paint, more machines to fix and keep running. And if you ever get rich enough to afford others to do all those things, then you have to worry about thieves, crooks, the Internal Revenue Service, and a host of other problems. How silly it is, then, to think that more land, a nicer house, more rooms, or finer furniture will make us happy. How sinful to plot and struggle and scratch and scrape in order to get all those things and lose sight of, and even title to, our inheritance in heaven. I feel sorry for people who think they have to work seven days a week to earn enough to pay for what they have or what they want. They miss getting together with God's people to get to know Jesus better just so they can get more. Jesus has something better in store for us than all that!

Only Jesus Christ can offer lasting happiness. He offers happiness that lasts even when the house you live in has wind whistling through the cracks, when the furniture is crates and boards, and when the yard gives you three or four feet of room from the next-door neighbor. This happiness frees us to enjoy what we have. Even more, it frees us to help those around us enjoy what they have instead of being unhappy that they have it. When our neighbor is in danger of losing his home or property, we can act out God's goodness by doing what we can to help our neighbor keep his possessions, even if we have to take a loss to do it! That's God's way!

When we help our neighbor hold onto his possessions, we are laying an offering of thanks on God's doorstep for all the good things he has given us in the name of Jesus. We can do that through various Christian relief agencies or fraternal societies. We can also help people right around us. For example, instead of rubbing our hands in glee at a bankruptcy sale, thinking we can get things at fire sale prices, we could sacrifice to help a person avoid going into bankruptcy. All we have comes from God. We are free to enjoy what he gives us and free to help our neighbor enjoy and keep what God has given him.

Prayer: Lord Jesus, we live in a world that is greedy. We are tempted to think that happiness is found in having more and more and more. We are also tempted to cheat or take advantage of those going through hard times to get their property or businesses. Forgive us when we begin sinfully to want what You have given as blessing to our neighbors. That means forgive us when we start thinking of ways we can get what belongs to someone else without giving him a fair price for it, or when we think of ways we can force our neighbor into giving or selling his possessions to us. Help us remember that we have an inheritance in heaven that can't be taxed, stolen, or ruined, so that when we remember this, we will be happy with what we have, and will be willing to help our neighbor enjoy what he has. Amen.

Object lesson: What kind of a house would you like to live in? Big? With your own bedroom? Your own bathroom? A big yard to play in?

Once there was a king named Ahab who lived in a big house. He had more rooms than a schoolhouse. He had a big yard. He owned large stables full of horses. But he wasn't happy. He had a neighbor named Naboth who owned a pretty garden of grapes called a vineyard. King Ahab offered to buy the garden, but Naboth didn't want to sell because it had been in his family for a long time. So, do you know what King Ahab did? He killed Naboth and stole Naboth's vineyard! Do you suppose this made Ahab happy? No. God sent a messenger named Elijah to condemn Ahab to death. Before a few weeks went by, before Ahab could have time to enjoy his stolen vineyard, he was killed in a war. What good did that vineyard and all those rooms and that big house and all those stables do Ahab then? Was he able to move into a better home after he was dead? No. He ended up living with the devil and his angels in a place worse than you or I can imagine.

Ahab should have thought more about where he was going to live forever than about where he was going to spend a few years on earth. We don't have to make Ahab's mistake. Whether you live in a small, crowded, ugly house, or in a big, roomy, pretty house someday, you are not going to live there for very long. Jesus has a place in heaven for you, with many rooms, a big place, to live in forever. We don't have to waste a lot of time and energy worrying about the kind of house we are living in here.

Deuteronomy 5:21
Philippians 2:1-4
Luke 12:1-15

10. The Tenth Commandment: Satisfaction

> **THE TENTH COMMANDMENT**
> Thou shalt not covet thy neighbor's wife, nor his manservant, nor his maidservant, nor his cattle, nor anything that is thy neighbor's. *What does this mean?* We should fear and love God that we may not estrange, force, or entice away from our neighbor his wife, servants, or cattle, but urge them to stay and do their duty.

When I was growing up, I heard people use the old saying, "The grass is always greener on the other side of the fence." It wasn't until I moved here, however, that I saw what this meant. Every once in a while, I will see some cow or horse, its head forced between two strands of barbed wire, munching on grass outside the pasture. Acres of the same kind of grass spread out behind it. How silly, right? Those animals will risk personal injury so that they can have more of what they already have in abundance.

People, even Christians, do the same kind of thing. How many people have thought that if they had a different husband or wife, they would be happier? Many adulterous affairs start because we are not satisfied with the spouse God gave us. How many people have envied the success of their neighbors? We tend to think, "It's not fair — I should have all that. I work harder. I deserve it more." In Bible times a man would think, "If only I had my neighbor's cattle, I would be rich." Or he might think, "I wish I had my neighbor's servants. They would work harder for me than the ones I have." Envy turns into covetousness. Soon we begin to wonder how we could get what our neighbor has.

One day, as the Lord Jesus was preaching about the kind of care the heavenly Father gives us, a man asked Jesus to settle a property dispute between the man and the man's brother. Jesus had just told the people that God takes better care of us than He does of sparrows and that he stands by those who are persecuted. Suddenly, this man calls out, "Teacher, tell my brother to divide the inheritance with me." Notice how he missed the point Jesus was trying to make. This man wanted happiness — who doesn't? — but he wanted it his way, not the way Jesus offered. Jesus seems to offer some "pie in the sky by and by" happiness. But this man seemed to think, "If God were really taking care of me, He would see to it my brother shares the inheritance with me." Jesus wants us to feel secure simply by knowing that our heavenly Father will give us what we need. This man, like too many people today, thought that he could only be secure if he had more property. Jesus replied with a warning: "Watch out! Be on your guard against all kinds of greed; a man's life does not consist in the abundance of his possessions."

Too many people learn this truth the hard way. He who thinks he should have the wife of his neighbor usually discovers how second and third marriages fail at a much higher rate than first marriages. The man who seduces the wife of another man ends up with a woman who can be seduced by still another man. The same is true for women who seduce husbands away from their wives. The businessman who offers a higher wage to a worker than what the worker is presently making so he can compete better with other businessmen has just hired a man whose loyalty belongs to the highest bidder. Many companies have done this and then lost the worker, and secrets he learned, to some other bidder. Nebraska offers "The Good Life" to people who cross into its borders. It's so good that banks fail, businesses go bankrupt, and people go to jail because they were living the good life at the expense of others.

The Lord Jesus wants us to be free of greed, not because He likes poor people. He wants us to be free of greed so we can have the abundant life He wants us to have. He has an idea of what it takes to make you and me really happy. The God who keeps track of the number of hairs on your head also keeps track of your needs and desires. The God who generously provides for worthless birds also generously provides us with a spouse partner and all those material blessings to make life enjoyable.

Greed is a form of fear. A greedy person is driven by fear about the future. A greedy person is afraid that God passes by with the really good things and leaves only what is second or third best. So, the greedy person decides he has to take care of himself. He calms his fears by working to collect the goods God gave to his neighbor. Jesus said, "Do not be afraid of those who kill the body and after that can do no more. But I will show you whom you should fear: Fear him who, after the killing of the body, has power to throw you into hell." Greedy people fear the wrong thing. They fear what can happen to them in this life instead of what will happen to them forever.

But we don't need to be afraid of what will happen to us forever. Our fear of God is because we respect His great, uncontrollable power, power that He chooses to use for our sake. If so, then how much less do we need fear what will happen to us in this life — especially when Jesus has promised that He came to give us an abundant life?

What is the abundant life Jesus has planned for us? He gives a woman to a man so that they can be one flesh. We can expect that, even if the two end up finding it hard to get along with each other, Jesus still has a great blessing in store for them if they stay together. Sometimes we need to go through hard times in order to find the blessing Jesus has in store for us. Sometimes, all those years of living with a person one ends up not liking helps make one better ready for something Jesus has in store for an individual.

Jesus also makes sure we can make a decent living. He doesn't guarantee we will be rich, only that we will have food and shelter. He does bless some more than others — and it has nothing to do with how hard they work, only on the goodness of Jesus. But over all that, Jesus offers us hope for the future. Covetousness comes from the desire to look after oneself. When Jesus gave us forgiveness of sins and eternal life He made it possible for us to be satisfied with what grass we have in our own pasture instead of hoping we can get what's in our neighbor's. We know how life is going to turn out. What freedom that gives us now to live in hope and confidence!

Prayer: Spirit of God and the Lord Jesus, help us believe that God will give us all good things in His good way and in His good time. Forgive us when we begin to look at what our neighbor has with envy and greed. Help us be satisfied with the man or woman God gives us as a spouse. Help us be satisfied with the jobs that He gives us. Fill our hearts with generosity and loyalty towards our neighbors so that there will be no room for greed and envy. Amen.

Exodus 20:4-6
Galatians 3:10-14
Matthew 5:17-20

11. The Close Of The Commandments: Grace And Every Blessing

> **THE CLOSE OF THE COMMANDMENTS**
> *What does God say of all these Commandments?* He says thus: I, the Lord, thy God, am a jealous God, visiting the iniquity of the fathers upon the children unto the third and fourth generation of them that hate Me, and showing mercy unto thousands of them that love Me and keep My Commandments. *What does this mean?* God threatens to punish all that transgress these commandments. Therefore we should fear His wrath and not act contrary to them. But He promises grace and every blessing to all that keep these Commandments. Therefore we should also love and trust in Him and willingly do according to His Commandments.

Are you holy enough? Are you right with God? Bible scholars count 613 commandments in the teachings of Moses. David in Psalm 15 reduced them to eleven; Isaiah shrunk them to six; Micah binds them into three; and Habakkuk reduces them all to one, namely, "The righteous shall live by faith." If we can keep this one commandment, then we will be holy enough, right with God.

First, let's review what it means to be righteous. The original meaning of the word "right" is "straight." "Let me get this right" means "let me get this straight." When I say I am going right to the store, I mean that I will go straight to the store, not going anywhere else. To act right means that one's behavior is as straight as God wants it to be. God's standard of straightness is His commandments. The opposite of someone who is righteous is someone who is crooked. Don't we talk about crooks and thieves? A crooked person behaves in a way that does not match the straight standards God sets.

Who is righteous according to God's commandments? One sin puts a kink or wrinkle in the straight line God expects. And it matters not if it is a big kink or wrinkle or a small one. Take the nicest person you know — is his behavior as straight as the commandments measure? No! The best of us and the worst of us — makes no difference — are crooked. Now, we might sit around comparing who is more crooked, more cursed, but so what? God has no room in heaven for anything that is crooked, as Paul writes to the Galatians: "Cursed is everyone who does not continue to do everything written in the Book of the Law."

And it doesn't matter if we live straight or right from here on. We still have the life we have lived up till now that is crooked. We can't straighten out the past by living straight from now on. And we can't straighten out the past for the same reason we can't straighten out a coathanger — we don't have the right tools or ability. Try straightening out a coathanger. You can't. We are like a coathanger — crooked and wrinkled. So, no matter how we behave, we can never get right with God. And so serious is sin, the Bible tells us if we hate God, his anger lasts long after our grandchildren are dead.

But the Bible tells of another way to be right with God: Jesus Christ straightens us out. First, Jesus takes us into Himself by baptism so that we can be painlessly executed for our sins along with Jesus when He died on a cross. Jesus then takes the kinks out of our lives with the same power God used to wake Jesus up after He died. "Jesus was crucified for our transgressions and raised for our justification." To justify something is the Latin way of saying "to straighten something out." The power to straighten us out is found in the work of the Holy Spirit, who uses the Word and sacraments of Jesus to create and build faith in us. The miracle of mercy is that God, through Jesus, straightens out those who trust Him. It is God who both helps us want to do what is right and then helps us do it.

That brings us to the second half of the statement, "The righteous shall live by faith." We know who the righteous are — those Jesus has straightened out (not those who behave properly). This is one of the most liberating sentences in the Bible. Notice, the Bible doesn't say, "The righteous shall live by keeping the Ten Commandments," or by following certain church rules; there are no rules for righteous living.

God couldn't care less how we behave! He cares about what we believe! If we think that we can live a right life by following rules, we fall back under the curse that comes whenever we sin and put a kink in our life. Rather, Jesus came to free us from the dead-end kind of life that tries to follow rules. "The righteous shall live by faith." Simply put, the person who trusts Jesus is doing the only right thing God wants him to do.

When Jesus said that one's righteousness must exceed that of the Pharisees and the teachers of the law, they were insulted. So they asked Jesus, "What must a man do to do the works of God?" Jesus said, "To do the works of God you must believe on him whom he has sent." Period. Jesus did not say, "Believe on him whom he sent and then make sure you tithe, and go to church and so forth." He said, "Believe on him whom he has sent." Period. And, remember, Jesus gives us the faith we need for believing on Jesus each time we hear His Word!

Of course, those who trust Jesus will behave differently than most everyone else. For example, if we trust Jesus, then we will naturally want to spend as much time as we can getting to know Him better through his Word and sacraments. If we take Jesus at His Word we will want to go to church, attend Bible studies, and spend time in personal and family devotions. After all, He promised that anyone who hears and keeps His Word will be blessed. And think of the opportunities we have that people didn't have in Bible times: we have our own personal Bibles, we have radios and tape players to listen to Christian music or teachings.

If we trust Jesus, we will do our best to follow His instructions, even if they seem hard or silly. How silly to put hard-earned money in a collection plate when one could have nice things or go on nice vacations, or to spend time teaching Sunday school or be on the church council or go to church or do other things for the church, when you could be doing things that are fun! But Jesus says if we do all those things we will be blessed and rewarded. Or, how can a bowl of water make a difference in a baby? How can a bit of bread and a sip of wine make a difference? But Jesus tells us that He forgives sins when we do those things.

We will even be able to do the impossible — forgive the unforgivable, trusting that Jesus will make it up to us. We will be able to make disciples of all nations. Jesus promises that whatever we tell others about Him will not be wasted but will always do what He wants it to do.

If we take Jesus at his Word we will take care of the needs of those around us, even if doing so means tightening our own belt. Jesus did not give us leftovers, but "made himself poor so we could become rich." To live by faith also means trusting that we will get what we need, even when times look bad, and even when death knocks on our door.

Prayer: Lord Jesus, You redeemed us from the curse of the law. That means You paid the price it took in order to set us free from the curse our sinfulness earned us. Forgive us whenever we fall back into thinking that our behavior is what matters, when we lose sight of the work You have done to straighten us out. Help us live in the mercy You have shown us by filling us with Your Spirit who will give us the faith we need to live in holiness. Amen.

Genesis 1:26-27
Matthew 19:1-6
Ephesians 2:1-10

12. The First Article: God Gave Me My Eyes And Ears

> THE APOSTLES' CREED — THE FIRST ARTICLE
> I believe in God the Father Almighty, Maker of heaven and earth. *What does this mean?* I believe that God has made me and all creatures; that He has given me my body and soul, eyes, ears, and all my members, my reason and all my senses, and still preserves them.

You might be asking, "What does creation have to do with Advent?" During Advent we remember how Jesus made His first advent into the world centuries ago. Advent is an old Roman word that means "come to." In the first advent, Jesus came to the world to take the sins of the world to a cross. This first advent won for us forgiveness of sins. The second advent is one we wait for. Jesus has promised to come back to the world again. This second advent will end history as we know it. The second advent of Jesus will put an end to the evil that now troubles us. So, what does creation have to do with Advent?

Both show the power of God the Father. Both involve Jesus. First, creation and Advent show the power of God. The opening verses of Genesis show God speaking and things happening, things so complex that they can't happen by accident. In six days, God the Father created an entire universe. As Dr. Martin Luther pointed out in his catechism, we believe that God has made me and all creatures; that He has given me my body and soul, eyes, ears, and all my members, my reason and all my senses.

Let's take a closer look at those words, "He has given me my body and soul, eyes, ears, and all my members." Carl Sagan, a famous astronomer and author who professed to have no belief in

God or the Bible, nevertheless recognized the complexity of the design of creation. In his book *The Dragons of Eden* (New York: Random House, 1977, 24-25) he described the complexity of a chromosome: "A single human chromosome contains twenty billion bits of information. How much information is twenty billion bits? What would be its equivalent, if it were written down in an ordinary printed book in modern human language?" Sagan notes that twenty billion bits would be about the same as three billion letters. Figuring that an average word contains six letters, the amount of information contained on one single chromosome is about 500 million words. Figuring that an average page of printed type contains 300 words, this same amount of information would equal nearly two million pages. If a single book were estimated to contain 500 pages, the amount of information carried on just one human chromosome would equal 4,000 books. What this analogy makes clear, says Sagan, is that a single chromosome contains a vast amount of information. It is also clear that a very large resource is required to make up such a complex and perfectly-functioning creature as a human being.

Now, that's one chromosome! We have 26 of these things! That means the instructions it takes for our chromosomes to turn dirt into a human would fill a library of one hundred four thousand books! Other creatures have more, some have less. The amazing detail and difference we see among all living creatures shows the creative genius of God the Father, rather than that all life accidentally "evolved" from bits of matter that randomly bumped together. To believe in evolution is like believing that a 104,000-book library was formed when all the letters were dumped on the ground!

The first advent of Jesus showed a similar display of power. God the Father created a human life in the Virgin Mary without the usual help of a human father. The man that was born, our Lord Jesus, was sinless and without the damage sin has done to our chromosomes. The second advent will be marked by a similar miracle, repeated billions of times, as God speaks to the dead bodies and re-creates them with bodies that are not of the ground. Jesus, who is the first to come back to life that way, has demonstrated how God can create a new kind of body.

Both creation and the first advent came about because God the Father sent Jesus, first to organize the world. Jesus was the Word spoken by the Father. Then, God the Father sent Jesus to save the world. Jesus was the Word made flesh by the Father. The Father has one more thing to say to us. Soon the Father will send Jesus, the living Word of God, back to earth to collect us and take us to a new life that lasts forever. This is according to the Word Jesus gave us that He would do this. And He is good for His Word.

This is good news to us. This Father, who planned the arrangement of atoms in the molecules in the DNA of your tiny chromosomes, as well as all the other creatures of the world, is still concerned about every detail of your life. Saint Paul promises that God works all things together for our good because we love Jesus. The God who planned out the order of this universe right down to tiny subatomic details has included in His plans how to turn the damage done by sin into blessing for His people. Through Jesus Christ, God the Father has created a new past for you by the forgiveness of sins. The Father is now creating a new future for you according to the Word Jesus gave us.

We are doubly blessed! The God who created me is re-creating me. This is true for all of you who trust Jesus. That's the first blessing. The second blessing is that Jesus is the Son of God the Father Almighty. Like Father, like Son! What Jesus did for us in His first advent and what He will do in his second advent shows why we can believe in God the Father Almighty, maker of heaven and earth!

Prayer: Heavenly Father, we thank You that for the sake of the Lord Jesus Christ, Your Son, our Lord, You created us and then re-created us after sin had claimed us. We thank You for the amazing detail You have created in this universe that proves how You can take care of each of us. As we consider the tiniest details that go into chromosomes and genes, help us remember how You have promised to work other details of our lives into something equally or more glorious than our human bodies. Amen.

Genesis 1:26-30
1 Timothy 6:6-10
Matthew 6:25-34

13. The First Article: God Provides For Me

> **THE APOSTLES' CREED — THE FIRST ARTICLE**
> I believe in God the Father Almighty, Maker of heaven and earth. *What does this mean?* I believe that God ... has given me ... also clothing and shoes, meat and drink, house and home, wife and children, fields, cattle, and all my goods; that He richly and daily provides me with all that I need to support this body and life; that He defends me against all danger, and guards and protects me from all evil.

"God richly and daily provides me with all that I need to support this body and life." Do you really believe that? After all, there are Christians in Somalia and Ethiopia and other places in the world starving to death right now. There are Christians in India and Africa who are wearing the same outfit they have been wearing for the last three years. Locally, grain is still selling for the same price it was fifty years ago. How can a farmer make a profit? Who's going under this year? Children in school are bothered because they can't talk the folks into buying designer jeans. "I can't go to school dressed like this! I look like a beggar." Where I came from, we used to talk about keeping up with the Joneses. If the Joneses got a new car, everyone had to get one. If they got a color television, everyone had to get one. Otherwise people would think you were poor. In the city, unlike the rural areas, it's socially unacceptable to look cheap. Fear of poverty has created a welfare state. Do you know who gets the most welfare? The middle class! The middle class allows itself to be taxed silly so we can have entitlements, farm programs, and other social welfare benefits.

This reminds me of a poem: Said the Robin to the Sparrow: "There is one thing I would really like to know, Why these anxious human beings rush about and worry so." Said the Sparrow to the Robin: "Friend, I think that it must be, That they have no heavenly Father such as cares for you and me."

Jesus promised that our heavenly Father will take care of us. "So do not worry, saying, 'What shall we eat?' or 'What shall we drink?' or 'What shall we wear?' For the pagans run after all these things, and your heavenly Father knows that you need them. But seek first His kingdom and His righteousness, and all these things will be given to you as well." When He first came to this world nearly 2000 years ago, Jesus was showing how God wants to take care of us. First, He wants to get rid of the sin that curses us to death. To those who seek the righteousness of God, He promises all the food and protection they will need.

Dr. Martin Luther teaches us to say, "I believe that God has given me also clothing and shoes, meat and drink, house and home, wife and children, fields, cattle, and all my goods; that He richly and daily provides me with all that I need to support this body and life; that He defends me against all danger and guards and protects me from all evil." The same God who sent Jesus to remove our sins, for Jesus' sake gives us all the good things we need to survive until Jesus comes again to take us to Himself.

The money and property you possess come from God, not from you. Two farmers can work just as hard, plant the same seed, use the same fertilizer, have the same soil, get the same amount of rain and still not harvest the same crop: one can get hailed out while the other doesn't. Same with those who punch a time clock. The doors of your shop could be closed tomorrow. God can work things so that you don't have a job there anymore — it happens every day. Don't count on things always being the way they have been. God may decide that the table He wants to put your food on will be in a different part of the country than where you now live. He may decide to dress you better or worse than what you are wearing now simply by arranging for you to have a different job, or no job at all.

But the same Father who sees to it that Jesus Christ takes care of your soul, will see to it that your body is cared for until Jesus can come again to get and take you to where He will provide eternal room and board. The heavenly Father who sees to it that birds are fed and who dresses weeds better than kings will do at least that much for you. If He spent the life of His Son to save your soul, won't He richly take care of your body, according to what He thinks you need! We don't have to worry about our standard of living! A man who has a layover at an airport does not go into the bathroom, frown at its decor, and start redecorating! Why? Because he doesn't live there. He has a home in another place. While he is away he will get by with only what he absolutely needs, to have more money with which to furnish his permanent home. Why do we Christians work hard at trying to make our life in this world more comfortable? This life is like the airport and we are on our way home. We should spend our energy on getting ready for our eternal reward, and not worry so much about the bare walls in the airport restrooms of this temporary life.

Prayer: Forgive us, Lord Jesus, for worrying about what we shall eat or drink or what we shall wear. Forgive us for confusing what we need with what we would like to have. Help us believe that for Your sake, the heavenly Father will provide all that we need to support our body and life, that He will protect us from evil and harm. When we don't get what we think we should have, help us be thankful for what we do have. Fill us with Your Spirit so we will be able to wait patiently in this life until You return to take us into the next life. Amen.

Exodus 33:12-23
1 Peter 1:3-9
Matthew 5:43-48

14. The First Article: God's Fatherly, Divine Goodness And Mercy

> **THE APOSTLES' CREED — THE FIRST ARTICLE**
> I believe in God the Father Almighty, Maker of heaven and earth. *What does this mean?* I believe that God has made me and all creatures; that He has given me my body and soul, eyes, ears, and all my members, my reason and all my senses, and still preserves them; also clothing and shoes, meat and drink, house and home, wife and children, fields, cattle, and all my goods; that He richly and daily provides me with all that I need to support this body and life; that He defends me against all danger, and guards and protects me from all evil; and all this purely out of fatherly, divine goodness and mercy, without any merit or worthiness in me.

The fact that many, many years have passed since the first advent of Jesus and we don't know how many will pass before His second advent can cause us to get lost in the worries of the present. The good news is that the same heavenly Father who sent Jesus, His only-begotten Son, to this world to save us from sin, death, and the power of the devil, is still our heavenly Father today. We focus on how this heavenly Father takes good care of us while we wait for Jesus to return, as Dr. Martin Luther summarizes in our catechism, "all this purely out of fatherly, divine goodness and mercy, without any merit or worthiness in me."

We get this idea from Bible passages like the one in Matthew's Gospel where Jesus says this about the heavenly Father: "You have heard that it was said, 'Love your neighbor and hate your enemy.'

But I tell you: Love your enemies and pray for those who persecute you, that you may be sons of your Father in heaven. He causes His sun to rise on the evil and the good, and sends rain on the righteous and the unrighteous. If you love those who love you, what reward will you get? Are not even the tax collectors doing that? And if you greet only your brothers, what are you doing more than others? Do not even pagans do that? Be perfect, therefore, as your heavenly Father is perfect." What a miracle Jesus describes about the heavenly Father!

How do people usually act when they have an enemy? Do we want to do good for our enemy or do we want somehow to make him suffer for being our enemy? At best, we usually have the idea, "Stay away from him." But that's not how our heavenly Father works. "He causes His sun to rise on the evil and the good, and sends rain on the righteous and the unrighteous." What good news is found in these words for sinners! God doesn't look on a farm and ask himself, "Does that guy go to church? Is he a disciple of my Son, Jesus? Does he deserve good things?" No. He looks down and says, "How much rain does that guy need to go with the sunshine I am sending today?" God didn't look on the whole history of humankind and ask, "Is anyone worth saving?" Instead, He sent His Son into human flesh to bear all peoples' sin, and be all peoples' Savior. All this, as the Apostle Paul writes in his letter to the Romans, "while we were yet sinners"! Yet this is the greatest act of the Father's divine goodness and mercy!

Jesus challenges us to show the same kind of goodness, especially to people we don't like. He reminds us that divine goodness and mercy isn't shown to people who deserve it, but is shown equally to all. If you deserve something good, then it's not mercy that you get it. Mercy is shown only to those who need it. God shows no mercy to those who deserve it, but shows it equally to all who need it. After all, who really deserves God's love? Us, because we are Christians? We are Christians because the Father showed us divine goodness and mercy in the first place, not because we had anything to do with it! The Father that takes care of us, even though we still sin, takes care of those people we don't like. If He takes care of His enemies, how much more will He take care of us while we wait for Jesus to return! How silly it is, then, to worry about how much money is in the checkbook, what the economy is going to do, where the next meal is coming from, and all the other things people worry about! Our Father in heaven will take care of us.

Prayer: Heavenly Father, source of all divine goodness and mercy, we thank You that You do not wait until we stop sinning before You will take care of us. We admit that we do not deserve anything from You but eternal punishment for our many sins. Help us believe that the same mercy You show to all people (without first checking to see if they believe in You or not) will surely take care of us who do believe in You with the help of Your Holy Spirit. While we wait for Jesus to come again, give us more faith than ever before to trust Your care. And help us to be as merciful to those around us as You are to us. Amen.

Object lesson: How many of you have ever been naughty? Do your mommies and daddies ever say, "Since you have been naughty, we have decided not to give you any more food, and you can't stay here with us anymore?" Do mommies and daddies only do good things for children when the children act nice, or do mommies and daddies take good care of you even when you have been bad?

You have a heavenly Father who will take care of you whether you are good or whether you are bad, because He loves you. He likes the good things you do, but when you are bad, He forgives you for Jesus' sake and sends you His Holy Spirit to help you be a better boy or girl. But even if you didn't ever do what was right, your Father in heaven would still take good care of you.

1 Chronicles 23:28-31
2 Corinthians 9:6-15
Luke 17:11-19

15. The First Article: My Duty To Thank And Praise

> THE APOSTLES' CREED — THE FIRST ARTICLE
> I believe in God the Father Almighty, Maker of heaven and earth. *What does this mean?* I believe that God has made me and all creatures; that He has given me my body and soul, eyes, ears, and all my members, my reason and all my senses, and still preserves them; also clothing and shoes, meat and drink, house and home, wife and children, fields, cattle, and all my goods; that He richly and daily provides me with all that I need to support this body and life; that He defends me against all danger, and guards and protects me from all evil; and all this purely out of fatherly, divine goodness and mercy, without any merit or worthiness in me; for all which it is my duty to thank and praise, to serve and obey Him. This is most certainly true.

How many times have parents told children, "Now, don't forget to say thank you"? Grandma gives little Junior some cookies and he starts to walk away. Mom says, "What do you say?" Junior turns around and says, "Thank you." Don't parents teach their children that saying thank you is a duty? Why would saying thank you be a duty? To answer that, think of those children who never learned to say thank you. They usually grow up unthankful complainers. People who learn to say thank you also learn to depend on others and trust them. It's a duty to say thank you because when we say thank you, we are forced to remember that someone else was good to us. The Bible teaches that it is our duty to say thank you to God.

This was acted out by the priests in the Old Testament times. Priests were professional thankers. At least twice a day the priests performed a thank-you ritual. The priests also did these rituals at every holiday burnt offering sacrifice. You can read about that in chapter 23 of 1 Chronicles. The people were also taught to offer sacrifices of thanksgiving. God got half the offering as it was burned up on an altar, and the priests got the other half, as God's representatives. The people of God have always made sure that we set aside some of our worship time to say thank you.

That's because we believe we have a heavenly Father who generously provides for us. Christians have always believed that it is our duty to thank God for all the good things we enjoy. And because God doesn't need flowers or cards or anything else, God's people have always believed that the proper way to say thank you to God is to invest some of their time, skills, and property in passing on the good news of salvation. This usually means time and money given in church service, especially money, because money buys time where you can't spend time yourself.

How about you; how thankful are you? A family sat down at the dinner table following church one Sunday. "The sermon was boring today," said the teenage son. "Yeah, could you believe how the pastor stumbled over the reading of the Scripture?" his sister chimed in. Mother said, "And the choir was terrible." Finally, father, showing his leadership, said, "Hush, you guys. Quit complaining. What did you expect for a buck?" Now, while this story illustrates how many Christians are cheap saying thank you with their cash, it also illustrates how Christians are cheap with giving of their time and talents in grateful service to Jesus as well. I believe that modern Christians have forgotten that it is their duty to support the work of their church richly — even at personal sacrifice of comfort and pleasure. I believe that too many Christians take Jesus Christ for granted. Too many Christians are like the husband who expects his meals to be cooked and his laundry to be washed and the house to be kept clean, but hardly ever gives of himself in gratitude to his wife.

Now, what kind of thankfulness shall we show? To answer that, ask yourself what the heavenly Father has done for you. Let's say that green is the color of thankfulness. Green shows life. Shall we be like the mighty maple or the humble pine? The mighty maple is green as long as it is warm. The humble pine is green all year long, even in the cold and dead of winter. Paul wrote to the Corinthians asking them to be generous in their green season to those who were in the winter of poverty, so that when the winter of want would come on the Corinthians, others would share their greenness with them. The more money you give for church work, the more your thank you matches the generosity of our heavenly Father. The more time you spend telling others about Jesus, the more your thank you matches the sacrifice of Jesus' whole life for you. The more you use your abilities to praise God, the more your thank you matches the creative power of God that made all your life possible. "Whoever sows sparingly will reap sparingly." May we be more like the grateful Samaritan leper Jesus cured than the nine Jews who didn't do their simple duty of saying thank you.

Prayer: Thank You, heavenly Father, for all the good things You send our way, especially when You sent Your Son Jesus to bear our sin and be our Savior. Forgive us for the cheap and grudging way we have said thank you, as well as all the times we have taken You and Jesus for granted. Give us generous hearts like Yours so that we can be part of Your generous hand in providing for the needs of the world around us, both the physical needs, as well as the spiritual needs. Amen.

Psalm 100
Colossians 1:15-20
Matthew 1:18-23

16. The Second Article: Begotten Of The Father From Eternity

> THE APOSTLES' CREED — THE SECOND ARTICLE
> I believe in Jesus Christ, His only Son, our Lord, who was conceived by the Holy Ghost, born of the Virgin Mary, suffered under Pontius Pilate, was crucified, dead, and buried; He descended into hell; the third day He rose again from the dead; He ascended into heaven, and sitteth on the right hand of God the Father Almighty; from thence He shall come to judge the quick and the dead. *What does this mean?* I believe that Jesus Christ ... purchased and won me ... not with gold or silver but with His holy, precious blood and with His innocent suffering and death.

Sherwood Wirt wrote the following in a Christmas card: "The people of that time were being heavily taxed, and faced every prospect of a sharp increase to cover expanding military expenses. The threat of world domination by a cruel, ungodly, power-intoxicated band of men was ever just below the threshold of consciousness. Moral deterioration had corrupted the upper levels of society and was moving rapidly into the broad base of the populace. Intense nationalistic feeling was clashing openly with new and sinister forms of imperialism. Conformity was the spirit of the age. Government handouts were being used with increasing lavishness to keep the population from rising up and throwing out the leaders. Interest rates were spiraling upward in the midst of an inflated economy. External religious observances were considered a political asset, and abnormal emphasis was being placed upon sports and athletic competition. Racial tensions were at the breaking point.

In such a time, and amid such a people, a child was born to a migrant couple who had just signed up for a fresh round of taxation, and who were soon to become political exiles. And the child who was born was called, among other things, Immanuel, God with us" (in Michael P. Green, ed., *Illustrations for Biblical Preaching*, Grand Rapids: Zondervan Publishing Company, 1990, 57-58).

God with us! God with us, in a real world of crime, corruption and corrosive competition! What a nice story to tell around the fireplace and put on Christmas cards. Those were the good old days.

Too bad we can't have God with us today. It surely would be nice. We face crime, corruption, and corrosive competition. Families break up every day. Teenage girls deliver babies that have no legal fathers, or worse, they kill the babies. Alcoholic men and women ruin families. Drug abuse visits the schoolhouse. Crooks and thieves control food supplies and other necessary goods. Our country used to be filled with people working hard to get ahead. Today, we have become a nation of couch potatoes getting a daily fix of sex, violence, and lust. In 1992 we elected a man as our national leader who had pledged to give homosexuality protected legal status. He had pledged to lift all restriction on abortion and to use tax money to pay for such a thing, including on our daughters who won't have to tell us first. Adultery, murder, lies, stealing, rebellion, and lust are now socially acceptable!

The good news is that we do have God with us today. "I believe in Jesus Christ, His only Son, our Lord, who was conceived by the Holy Ghost, born of the Virgin Mary, suffered under Pontius Pilate, was crucified, dead, and buried; He descended into hell; the third day He rose again from the dead; He ascended into heaven and sitteth on the right hand of God the Father Almighty; from thence He shall come to judge the quick and the dead. What does this mean? I believe that Jesus Christ, true God, begotten of the Father from eternity ... is my Lord." By these words we proclaim that God is with us today in the person and work of Jesus Christ.

A messenger from heaven interrupted the dream one night of a certain Joseph of Nazareth. "Joseph, son of David, do not be afraid to take Mary home as your wife, because what is conceived in her is from the Holy Spirit. She will give birth to a son and you will call his name Jesus, because he will save his people from their sins."

Three parts of what the messenger said shows us that Jesus is God with us. First, "that which is conceived in her is from the Holy Spirit." Most children come from the union of a man and a woman. Jesus came from the life-giving work of the Spirit on Mary, with no help from a man. This marks him as God's Son. The name "Jesus" underlines who Jesus is. "Jehovah Saves" is the meaning of the name Jesus. "He will save his people from their sins." The Bible is full of saviors: Moses, Gideon, David, Abraham, Deborah, and a host of others. But none of them saved people from sins. Only God can save someone from sins. Jesus, therefore, had to be the Lord the prophets had long spoken of.

The catechism sums this all up with the words, "begotten from the Father from all eternity." "Begotten" is a word used by kings to point out who was to take over when the king retired or died. Psalm 2:7 puts these words in the mouth of Jesus: "I will proclaim the decree of the LORD: He said to me, 'You are my Son; today I have begotten you.' " The rest of the psalm describes how this Son of God would be eternal king. Psalm 110 teaches us that this king is still with us today. Paul reminds the Colossians that in Jesus, the fullness of God chose to dwell in bodily form. Since Jesus rose from the dead and ascended into heaven, He has been with us as Savior from sin and evil, according to His promise to be with us till the close of the age. God is with us and his name is Jesus!

Prayer: Lord Jesus, help us! We are surrounded by more evil than we can describe. Sin assaults us on all sides, including from inside us. We are like driftwood carried along on a flood of evil, powerless to stop the crime and corruption around us. Death knocks on our doors daily, claiming loved ones or threatening others. Devils fill the world with hate and work to destroy those who belong to You. As we remember Your birth, help us believe that disguised in that baby born in a barn was the full power of God that created the universe. Help us to believe that You will save us from sin, death, and the power of the devil because You are God Almighty who clothed Yourself in human flesh. Amen.

Genesis 3:14-15
Hebrews 2:10
Luke 3:23-38

17. The Second Article: Jesus Born Of The Virgin Mary Is My Lord

> THE APOSTLES' CREED — THE SECOND ARTICLE
> I believe in Jesus Christ, His only Son, our Lord, who was conceived by the Holy Ghost, born of the Virgin Mary, suffered under Pontius Pilate, was crucified, dead, and buried; He descended into hell; the third day He rose again from the dead; He ascended into heaven, and sitteth on the right hand of God the Father Almighty; from thence He shall come to judge the quick and the dead. *What does this mean?* I believe that Jesus Christ, true God, begotten of the Father from eternity, and also true man, born of the Virgin Mary, is my Lord....

In the early days of the Christian church, two false doctrines quickly sprang up. The first was that Jesus Christ was only a man, because God was too big and too unlike us to fit inside Jesus. The second false teaching was that Jesus was God, but not really human, and for the same reasons. The second false teaching claimed that people saw what only looked and felt like the shape of a man, a kind of three-dimensional hallucination. Both of these heresies had a hard time understanding the human nature of Jesus. They asked the question, "How can God be a man?" The answer heretics gave was, "God can't."

Some people still talk this way today. Jehovah's Witnesses are at the top of the pile. They teach that Jesus was a man who was given godlike abilities, but that's all. Mormons also teach that Jesus is really only a man who has godlike powers. They also teach that God the Father is really only a super man. They also teach that all men will eventually become gods if they are good Mormons, and the women will join their men if they kept their men happy. Other cults have similar teachings.

How can God be a man? Some people think that God is infinite and Jesus is just a speck of dust on a speck of a world in an infinite universe. They ask, how could the infinite God fit into such a tiny nothing? Some people think that God can no more fit inside Jesus than you can pack all your family's clothes into one suitcase to go on vacation! So, if Jesus is God, some say He could not be a real man.

The Bible, however, is clear. Jesus *is* God, completely and fully. And He *is* a real man. Matthew and Luke go to great pains to show that Jesus has a human background. Luke's account is the most complete. Luke shows that Jesus is a son of Adam, just like you and me. Furthermore, if you look at the list of names, 41 nobodies fill the list between Jesus and King David. The ancestry of David is filled with crooks, killers, idolaters, sex perverts, and other ordinary sinners. If anything, the ancestry of Jesus shows him to be so human, we might wonder how He could be God!

But, God became a man! What a miracle! All that is God can be found in Jesus! The God who created the universe is the man Jesus. The God who broke the power of sin is the man Jesus. The God who rules the universe for the sake of the church is the man Jesus. He has the name that is above every name, that at the name of Jesus every knee shall bend in heaven, on earth, and beneath the earth. Only one person can claim that kind of honor: God, and Jesus the man has it too.

People of old expected God to become a man. In Psalm 22, which the writer of the letter to the Hebrews quotes, Jesus calls us brothers. But even more important, we learn from the letter to the Hebrews that God had to become a man so that He could die and thereby break the power of death. I remember being told not to eat raw bread dough because it would continue to expand in my stomach until it would burst my stomach. That's what happened to death. Death swallowed Jesus, but forgot that God was wrapped in that human flesh. Once in the grave, Jesus swelled to His full divine size and literally popped the lid off His grave. God became a man so that He could be bait in a trap that would destroy our enemies.

One other benefit of God becoming a man is found in another place in the letter to the Hebrews. Because God became a man, we now have a high priest who prays for us, who knows what it feels like to be a human living in a world ruined by sin. He has been touched by that evil. He, who is above all evil, became human so He could be touched by evil. Now He can be especially sympathetic with us in our sufferings.

"Born of the Virgin Mary." How simply these words summarize the miracle of the birth of Jesus. That God would be born of a woman! How can this be? Can an ant explain how sound can be turned into radio waves and sent a million miles away? All I know is that this man Jesus is my Lord. He takes care of me and saves me from human misery. I pray that He is your Lord as well.

Prayer: Lord Jesus, God of all power and might, yet man of sorrow and grief: thank You for taking on human flesh in order to save us from sin, death, and the power of the devil. Give us faith to trust that Your human nature does not limit Your ability to use Your full divine abilities on our behalf. Help us to believe that You, the man, are with us; that You, the man, offer Your body and blood to us to eat and drink for forgiveness. Help us to believe that You, the man, will someday soon come to take us to live with You forever. Amen.

Daniel 3:19
1 Corinthians 12:1-3
John 20:24-29

18. The Second Article: Jesus Is My Lord

> THE APOSTLES' CREED — THE SECOND ARTICLE
> And in Jesus Christ, His only Son, our Lord, who was conceived by the Holy Ghost, born of the Virgin Mary, suffered under Pontius Pilate, was crucified, dead, and buried; He descended into hell; the third day He rose again from the dead; He ascended into heaven, and sitteth on the right hand of God the Father Almighty; from thence He shall come to judge the quick and the dead. *What does this mean?* I believe that Jesus Christ, true God, begotten of the Father from eternity, and also true man, born of the Virgin Mary, is my Lord....

In the days shortly after Jesus ascended into heaven, Christians quickly found themselves in the political doghouse. Jews hated them because Christians dared worship as Lord and master of human destiny a rabbi who had died on a cursed tree. Everyone else hated them because Christians had the treasonous idea that a Jew named Jesus was Lord instead of Emperor Caesar. Anyone who believed in Jesus ran great risks. He could lose his job. He could be shunned by others in the community. His family could disown him. This was especially true if a Christian came from a Jewish family. To this day, many Jewish families hold a funeral for anyone who converts to Christianity. But if a person was willing to say, "Jesus is cursed," he would be let back into the community. If he would say, "Caesar is Lord," he could get his job back, or be set free from prison.

"Jesus is Lord." These words still separate the world into two camps. One camp grinds its teeth in anger when it hears those words.

"Jesus is not Lord," they cry. While they cannot agree among themselves who they think is Lord, they all agree that Jesus isn't. And most of them agree that anyone who says, "Jesus is Lord," is at least stupid and at worst dangerous. People in the "Jesus is not Lord" camp include those who ridicule Jesus in public or who chase Christians out of public life.

Their battle cry is summed up in the words, "Jesus is cursed." The founder of the Soviet empire declared that Jesus is a curse on the world. People like television producer Norman Lear consider Jesus to be a curse in our country. Modern enemies of Jesus have said that Jesus Christ and His ragtag band of bloodthirsty barbarians have been a curse on civilization, the root of most wars, and a blight on history. We should not be surprised that laws are being passed to limit the expression of Christian faith in public, starting with nativity scenes at the city hall to prayers at graduations.

One other camp rallies around the words, "Jesus is Lord." We are convinced that Jesus of Nazareth is also Lord Jehovah. We are convinced that the baby born in a Bethlehem barn to a virgin named Mary now sits at the right hand of God the Father Almighty, as King of kings and Lord of lords. Burn us at the stake, chop off our heads, tax us, muzzle us, throw us out of society — but we won't change our minds.

Are we crazy? Why should we believe the stories of the Bible? What makes the Bible different than the Koran, or the holy books of the Hindus or the Buddhists? Saint Paul reminds us why we believe Jesus is Lord. "No one who is speaking by the Spirit of God says, 'Jesus is cursed,' and no one can say, 'Jesus is Lord,' except by the Holy Spirit."

Wouldn't it be nice if we could have been eyewitnesses to the things the Bible says Peter, James, and John saw? Wouldn't it be nice to take Thomas' place, whom the Bible says was able to put his fingers in the holes made by the nails and spear? Wouldn't it be nice if we could see Jesus go nose to nose with these smart aleck news show anchors? It seems so unfair that we do not get to see Jesus, but have to rely on the words written in a book. But faith in Jesus is not based on experience or feelings. Many, many people saw Jesus, and did not believe in Him. Faith in Jesus is created in us by the Holy Spirit.

The Holy Spirit has a big job cut out for Him if He is going to make us believe in Jesus. The only help we get in saying that Jesus is Lord comes from the Holy Spirit. That Spirit is poured out in baptism, Saint Paul tells us in His letter to Titus. The faith we need to believe in Jesus comes from hearing the words which the Holy Spirit inspired prophets and apostles to write down, Saint Peter tells us. Holy Communion, Saint Paul tells us in his first letter to the Corinthians, is the message of Jesus acted out. Paper, ink, bread, wine, and water are taken up by God's Spirit and forged into tools of faith. So, if we are going to continue to be able to say, "Jesus is Lord," we must continue to be blown along by God's Spirit as He comes to us in the Word and sacraments God has given us.

Prayer: Lord Jesus, we regret that we must once again confess that we do not love Your Word and sacraments as we should. We are easily drawn away from them by other interests and by pressure our culture puts on us to renounce You. Give us faith to come closer to Your Word and sacraments so that we will not compromise with the world, or worse, slip into joining unbelievers in cursing You by our lips or by our deeds. Help us really believe that You are Lord so that we will not fear what the devil or the world around us can do to us. Stand us tall as witnesses of the power of Your Spirit to change lives. Amen.

Deuteronomy 15:12-15
Hebrews 9:11-15
Luke 2:25-38

19. The Second Article: Jesus Christ Redeemed Me

> **THE APOSTLES' CREED — THE SECOND ARTICLE**
> I believe in Jesus Christ, His only Son, our Lord, who was conceived by the Holy Ghost, born of the Virgin Mary, suffered under Pontius Pilate, was crucified, dead, and buried; He descended into hell; the third day He rose again from the dead; He ascended into heaven, and sitteth on the right hand of God the Father Almighty; from thence He shall come to judge the quick and the dead. *What does this mean?* I believe that Jesus Christ ... redeemed me....

In the letter to the Hebrews we read, "When Christ came as high priest of the good things that are already here, he went through the greater and more perfect tabernacle that is not man-made, that is to say, not a part of this creation. He did not enter by means of the blood of goats and calves; but he entered the Most Holy Place once for all by his own blood, having obtained eternal redemption." What is redemption? Supermarkets give out redemption stamps. You take the stamps and stick them in stamp books. Then you trade in stamp books for a toaster or other household goods. This transaction has two parts: purchasing the right of redemption and then claiming your merchandise. You buy the right of redemption when you make your original purchase, and the store gives you the stamps as a token. Later you take the stamps to the redemption center and use them to claim something you want. Those items you redeem are not free, because in reality you already paid the price for them when you made your original purchase.

In a similar way, Jesus Christ obtained eternal redemption when He died on the cross. That means that his life was the price He paid in order to buy what He wanted. The Bible gives us an idea of what it means that Jesus redeemed us. In the book of Deuteronomy we learn that if a person had to sell himself into slavery in order to pay debts off, he had to be set free after six years. Not only so, but his master had to give him commodities to start his freedom with. God explained why: "Remember that you were slaves in Egypt and the LORD your God redeemed you." When Moses led God's rescue of the Hebrews from Egypt, God was really redeeming them. Redemption set a person free from slavery. The price paid to set the Hebrews free was the firstborn of man and beast not protected by the blood of the passover lamb. So, even if no money changed hands, when a slave was set free from his debt, he was redeemed from slavery.

We have been redeemed by the blood of Jesus. How often do we hear that without really stopping to think what that means! It means that Jesus had to die in order to set us free from the debtors' prison run by the devil! Think of all the wars we have fought where the price paid to liberate some country from an invader was the lives of Americans and their allies.

There was a young boy who lived in a New England seaport and loved to watch the boats come in from their daily catch. One day he decided to build a little sailboat all on his own. He worked for weeks, making sure each detail was just right. Finally the big day arrived. He went down to the wharf and proudly put his boat into the water. As he triumphantly observed his new sailboat, he noticed that the wind had suddenly changed, and the tiny boat was being swept out of sight. The little boy was heartbroken. Every day for a month he went back to see if his boat had been washed up on shore.

Finally, one day in the market he saw his boat in a store window. He excitedly ran into the store and told the proprietress that it was his boat. The woman only responded by saying that the boat would cost him two dollars. After pleading with her to no avail, the boy finally pulled out the money and gave it to the store owner. As the boy was leaving the store, he said, "Little boat, you are twice mine. You are mine because I made you, and now you are mine because I bought you."

This is what Jesus did for us when he died. He who created us sacrificed His life in order to own us again after we had strayed into the devil's possession. We are twice His! Now He can do with us what He wanted to do in the first place, as we learn from the letter to the Hebrews: "How much more, then, will the blood of Christ, who through the eternal Spirit offered Himself unblemished to God, cleanse our consciences from acts that lead to death, so that we may serve the living God!" The final result of redemption is a new life. It is a life serving God. And in case you might think that this means being a slave to a new master, the next words from that letter should put your hearts at ease: "For this reason Christ is the mediator of a new covenant, that those who are called may receive the promised eternal inheritance — now that He has died as a ransom to set them free from the sins committed under the first covenant." Our new life of service involves an eternal inheritance! God grant us faith to live up to our redemption!

Prayer: Lord Jesus, blessed Redeemer, Savior and friend! Words are not enough to say what a blessing You have given us when You died to set us free from our sins! Help us believe in our redemption so that we will live the holy lives You have planned for us. Forgive us when we live as if we were still slaves to the devil. Amen.

2 Samuel 7:18-24
Colossians 1:1-14
Luke 24:13-27

20. The Second Article: Lost And Condemned

> **THE APOSTLES' CREED — THE SECOND ARTICLE**
> I believe in Jesus Christ, His only Son, our Lord, who was conceived by the Holy Ghost, born of the Virgin Mary, suffered under Pontius Pilate, was crucified, dead, and buried; He descended into hell; the third day He rose again from the dead; He ascended into heaven, and sitteth on the right hand of God the Father Almighty; from thence He shall come to judge the quick and the dead. *What does this mean?* I believe that Jesus Christ ... has redeemed me, a lost and condemned creature....

A pastor of a church in Boston met a young boy in front of the sanctuary. The boy was carrying a rusty cage in which several birds fluttered nervously. The pastor inquired, "Son, where did you get those birds?" "I trapped them out in the field," the boy replied. "What are you going to do with them?" "I'm going to play with them, and then I guess I'll just feed them to an old cat we have at home." When the pastor offered to buy them, the lad exclaimed, "Mister, you don't want them, they're just little old wild birds and can't sing very well." The pastor replied, "I'll give you two dollars for the cage and the birds." "Okay, it's a deal, but you're making a bad bargain." The exchange was made, and the boy went away whistling, happy with his shiny coins. The pastor walked around to the back of the church property, opened the door of the small wire cage, and let the struggling creatures soar into the blue. The next Sunday he took the empty cage into the pulpit and used it to illustrate Christ's coming to seek and to save those who like the birds were destined for destruction. This illustrates what it means that Jesus "redeemed me, a lost and condemned creature."

Like the birds the boy caught, the devil had us in his cage. In Paul's letter to the Colossians, he calls this cage "the dominion of darkness." The very name brings up a gloomy picture in my mind. Darkness! The last few months have been cloudy and gloomy for us, but never dark. Dark is like the dust storms that some of you have seen. Days and days of gloomy grayness are bad enough. But days and days of darkness — ask the people who live in Antarctica or near the North Pole what weeks and weeks of darkness will do to morale. And that's not as bad as the kingdom of darkness. The devil's home is a place of "outer darkness," according to Jesus. In that darkness there is weeping and gnashing of teeth, much worse than you have ever heard at any funeral. The devil's darkness is darker than death and the pain and sorrow death causes. It is a place for lost and condemned sinners to spend eternity. Those trapped in the devil's darkness would find death a relief, and yet they never get it.

The Lord saw what we would have forever. So the Father set in motion a plan. Saint Paul wrote, "[He] qualified you to share in the inheritance of the saints in the kingdom of light. For he has rescued us from the dominion of darkness and brought us into the kingdom of the Son he loves, in whom we have redemption, the forgiveness of sins." God's plan set up a kingdom of light for us to inherit. How refreshed we are when we see the sun again after days of gloomy cloudiness. How much greater the joy the Father has in store for us when He brings us from the valley of the shadow of death into the kingdom of light!

But no one was qualified to live in that kingdom. What sinner can see the face of God and live? The sins that trapped us in the devil's darkness made it impossible for us to survive in the light. So the Father set about to fix that. He got us out of the darkness when he "rescued us from the dominion of darkness and brought us into the kingdom of the Son he loves, in whom we have redemption, the forgiveness of sins." Jesus, who is the light who came into the world, draws us into His kingdom of light. He brings us into His kingdom of light, rescuing us from darkness, by redeeming us.

But remember, redemption means paying a price to set someone free. The price Jesus Christ paid to set us free from the devil's dark kingdom was the price of His own life. When Jesus died, He raided the devil's dark valley of the shadow of death and turned lost and condemned sinners loose. Those who follow Jesus back to the light leave behind their sins in the grave of Jesus. We can follow Jesus because He has joined us to Himself in baptism, so that as He rose from the dead, we too might walk in newness of life. As long as we stay close to Jesus, He keeps us clean of sin and keeps His light shining in us. That is why the apostle says, about Jesus, "in whom we have redemption, the forgiveness of sins." Forgiveness of sins shows we are free from our former life, just as redeeming a slave set him free from his past debts.

Jesus redeemed me, a lost and condemned creature. I am free to serve Him in thanksgiving, doing what is pleasing to Him. Join me in getting to know that life better.

Prayer: We always thank You, God, the Father of our Lord Jesus Christ, because of the faith You have given us in Christ Jesus and of the love You have created in us for all the saints — the faith and love that spring from the hope that is stored up for us in heaven and that You have already told us about in the Word of truth, the gospel that has come from You. We pray that we may live a life worthy of the Lord and may please Him in every way, such as bearing fruit in every good work, growing in the knowledge of God, being strengthened with all power according to His glorious might, and joyfully giving thanks to You, Father, who has qualified us to share in the inheritance of the saints in the kingdom of light. Amen.

Numbers 18:15-17
1 Peter 1:13-19
Mark 10:35-45

21. The Second Article: Jesus Purchased And Won Me

> **THE APOSTLES' CREED — THE SECOND ARTICLE**
> I believe in Jesus Christ, His only Son, our Lord, who was conceived by the Holy Ghost, born of the Virgin Mary, suffered under Pontius Pilate, was crucified, dead, and buried; He descended into hell; the third day He rose again from the dead; He ascended into heaven, and sitteth on the right hand of God the Father Almighty; from thence He shall come to judge the quick and the dead. *What does this mean?* I believe that Jesus Christ ... purchased and won me ... not with gold or silver but with His holy, precious blood and with His innocent suffering and death.

We have a story from the Gospel of Mark about Jesus that helps us understand those words, "purchased and won me ... not with gold or silver but with his holy, precious blood and with his innocent suffering and death." It seems the disciples figured that Jesus was about to set up some kind of kingdom. James and John wanted to be top advisors in that kingdom. They asked to sit at Jesus' left and right. Little did they know what that really meant! Jesus told them that those places were already reserved for others — and it turned out that they were reserved for the two thieves who were crucified with Jesus.

Jesus then gave the main qualification for a high position in His kingdom: "Whoever wants to be great among you must be your servant, and whoever wants to be first must be slave of all. For even the Son of man did not come to be served, but to serve and to give his life as a ransom for many." These words help us understand the value of Jesus.

By the way, in the Bible, the words "redemption" and "ransom" mean the same thing. The Greek word Jesus used was the word people used when they talked about paying a price to set someone free. But ransom means more to us than redemption. How many people talk about redeeming a person? But we understand what it means to ransom a person. Ransom is the price paid to set a person free from captivity. The price Jesus paid to set us free was His life. He did not spend cash to free us from sin, death, and the power of the devil. Gold or silver have value in themselves, apart from the person spending them. So, Jesus didn't spend the energy of humans or angels. He spent His life as the ransom to set us free.

In Bible times, redemption, or ransom, was the normal way to get a person out of hock. If a person owed money, he and his family could be sold into slavery to get back some of the money he owed. Family or friends, however, could pay the debt. Or a man could buy his freedom back by working it off. When Jesus said that He came not to be served, but to serve and give His life as a ransom for many, He is going one step further than merely paying off the debt. He became a slave whose chief job was to go on a miserable and messy suicide mission that would ransom humankind from the devil. A famous street missionary from the last century, D. L. Moody, once said, "The measure of a man is not how many servants he has, but how many men he serves." How much does that make Jesus Christ worth? No wonder He was given the name that is above every name, that at the name of Jesus, every knee in heaven, on earth, and beneath it would bow!

We can be great in the kingdom of heaven also. The story is told of two brothers who grew up on a farm. One went away to college, earned a law degree, and became a partner in a prominent law firm in the state capital. The other brother stayed on the family farm. One day the lawyer came and visited his brother, the farmer. He asked, "Why don't you go out and make a name for yourself and hold your head up high in the world like me?" The brother pointed and said, "See that field of wheat over there? Look closely. Only the empty heads stand up. Those that are well-filled always bow low." Said differently, "The branch that bears the most fruit is bent the lowest to the ground."

True greatness comes from putting others first. Jesus put you and me first, even though we weren't even born yet. That made Him great ... and also made us great. Think about it. If Jesus is God, and He put us first, doesn't that make us greater than God? And yet, by doing that, Jesus became the greatest. That sets up an interesting contest. To win first place, we must help everyone else win first place! We get ahead when we help others get ahead. Victory comes to him who loses the most. Jesus Christ came to serve and give His life as a ransom for many. We can't ransom anyone, because that job is already done. But there are plenty of openings in God's kingdom for slaves! We have freedom, now, to apply for those positions. Remember, only free people can have the freedom to become slaves if they want to.

Prayer: Lord Jesus Christ, You who became a slave so we could be set free, give us souls that are willing to die as slaves in service to others. Help us be willing to give up our rights so that we will be ready to take the abuse slaves take. Help us live in the freedom You won for us that allows us freely to sacrifice our own interests so that others may know of Your love and mercy. Amen.

Psalm 74:1-12
Revelation 5:1-10
Luke 4:31-41

22. The Second Article: Protected From The Devil's Power

> **THE APOSTLES' CREED — THE SECOND ARTICLE**
> I believe in Jesus Christ, His only Son, our Lord, who was conceived by the Holy Ghost, born of the Virgin Mary, suffered under Pontius Pilate, was crucified, dead, and buried; He descended into hell; the third day He rose again from the dead; He ascended into heaven, and sitteth on the right hand of God the Father Almighty; from thence He shall come to judge the quick and the dead. *What does this mean?* I believe that Jesus Christ ... has ... purchased and won me from all sins, from death, and from the power of the devil.

The power of the devil is great. His influence is felt everywhere. He would ruin the church if he could. Consider the story that is told about Jesus, how one day while He was in church, a man possessed by a demon jumped up and screamed, "What do you want with us, Jesus of Nazareth? Have you come to destroy us? I know who you are — the Holy One of God!" This demon challenged Jesus! Shouldn't the church be safe from the devil? Shouldn't we be free to meet and worship God without wondering if demons might be sharing the same room with us? If the church is not safe from the devil, where is it safe?

But that same story shows us that the church is safe from the devil. "Be quiet," Jesus said sternly. "Come out of him!" Then the demon threw the man down before them all and came out without injuring him. All the people were amazed and said to each other, "What is this teaching? With authority and power he gives orders to evil spirits and they come out!"

Jesus' power over sin goes further than casting out demons. He heals the sick mother-in-law of His friend and disciple Peter. Wherever Jesus went it was the same story. "He went around doing good and healing all who were under the power of the devil, because God was with him."

Jesus' enemies believed that Jesus was really the devil in disguise. If Jesus were the devil himself, they thought, that would explain why Jesus could boss evil around. But it wouldn't explain why Jesus allowed Himself to be crucified. The kind of power Jesus showed would have been more than enough to stop the Jews and the Romans from lynching Him. Satan's style is to use strength and power to get His way. Satan considers God to be a wimp because God doesn't force us to do things His way. Satan's way is to threaten people, make them live in fear, and cruelly crack down on disobedience. So the shame Jesus endured and the death Jesus died is more like something the devil would do to a person than what he would allow to be done to himself. So the fact that Jesus was crucified shows He wasn't working for or with the devil.

But if Jesus had only died on that cross, we could have said that He was a mighty hero who stood up to evil but could not stand up to the prince of evil. However, we know from eyewitness accounts that Jesus rose again from the dead. That shows us that Jesus is more powerful than the devil. Jesus is stronger than death, the devil's greatest strength. The devil has no claim on us because Jesus owns us now. Jesus robbed the devil in a daring daytime raid that was launched from a Roman cross. We have been purchased by Jesus and set free from slavery to sin, death, and the power of the devil. Jesus also won us from sin, death, and the power of the devil by His victory over the grave.

The Christian's view of Satan should be like that of a father at a zoo watching a lion roaring and pacing in his cage rather than that of his little boy, who was scared silly. Our fierce enemy is like a caged lion. Oh yes, he still walks about seeking whom he may devour, but he can't hurt us because Jesus is with us. We belong to Jesus now, and He takes care of what belongs to Him.

Prayer: Lord Jesus, by Your suffering and death You purchased our freedom from the debt of death we owed and won us as a prize from the devil's hoard of damned souls. Help us believe that You will not allow the devil, death, or sin to win us back. Help us to stand up to his roaring with faith in Your mercy and forgiveness. Make us holy so that the devil will be less able to use our consciences against us. Help us live like trophies worthy of the honor You have given us. Amen.

Object lesson: Did you ever have a bully bother you? A friend once related this experience to me. Once, when he was a boy, a bully named Andrew used to pick on him. He hit him, pushed him around, teased him, and made him very unhappy. He sometimes liked to hide behind bushes or trees and jump out at him as he walked by. Then one day, my friend noticed that Andrew was watching him as he walked past him after school. He noticed that he followed him home. My friend kept waiting for the bully to do something, but he never did. In fact, he never bothered him again. Just like that. All of a sudden. Many years later my friend found out why. His mom told him that she saw Andrew riding his bike. So she came out of the house and stopped him on the sidewalk. Smiling to Andrew, she said, "If you ever pick on my son again, I'll take you in my garage and paddle you. And if anyone else bothers him, I'll think you told him to do it, so I'll punish you." That's why Andrew started following him home — to make sure that no one else picked on him after school.

What is the name of an invisible bully that wants to bother us? The devil. Who is our friend that will protect us? Jesus! Just as my friend had a mom who looked out for him, we have a heavenly Father who looks out for us. He sent Jesus to protect us. Just as his mom was stronger than the bully, Jesus Christ is stronger than the devil. Jesus will see to it that the devil won't hurt you.

Deuteronomy 26:16-19
Revelation 1:1-8
Matthew 25:31-40

23. The Second Article: A New Purpose In Life

> **THE APOSTLES' CREED — THE SECOND ARTICLE**
> I believe in Jesus Christ, His only Son, our Lord, who was conceived by the Holy Ghost, born of the Virgin Mary, suffered under Pontius Pilate, was crucified, dead, and buried; He descended into hell; the third day He rose again from the dead; He ascended into heaven, and sitteth on the right hand of God the Father Almighty; from thence He shall come to judge the quick and the dead. *What does this mean?* I believe that Jesus Christ ... has redeemed me ... that I may be His own....

Fifteen hundred years before the death of Jesus, God had this to say to the Hebrew nation of Israel, "The LORD has declared this day that you are his people, his treasured possession as he promised, and that you are to keep all his commands." Moses spoke these words a short time before those Hebrews crossed the River Jordan and began taking possession of the land God had promised over 400 years earlier to a wandering Aramean named Abraham. Once again, God reminded the people that He had redeemed them from slavery in Egypt to be His own family.

Redemption, or ransom as we would call it today, rescued a person from captivity so he could be free to return to his family. The Egyptians paid a terrible price to ransom the Hebrews. Their nation was devastated by a series of judgments from God, the last of which cost them the firstborn of all male men and beasts. With that price, God purchased the freedom of the Israelites. That act of redemption set the Hebrews free to be God's people once again.

Like everything that happened to the people of God in the olden days before Jesus, all this tells us about Jesus Christ. God ransomed the Hebrew slaves from Egypt as a prophecy of what Jesus Christ came to do 1500 years later. The prophecy was fulfilled when God spent His firstborn Son in order to ransom all humankind from slavery to the devil. But He ransomed us for a purpose. We are not set free and left on our own. Negro slaves set free after the bloody American Civil War of the last century did not suddenly find that life got better. In fact, for most, life got worse. Former slaves lost their livelihood. They lost their homes. Many found themselves out on the streets trying to make ends meet. One hundred thirty years later, the blacks are still behind the majority of people in this country in enjoying the fruits of freedom. Jesus Christ, however, did not set us free from sin, death, and the power of the devil, and then expect us to be on our own. He set us free to be His own.

What does it mean to belong to Jesus? Jesus tells us, "When the Son of man comes in his glory, and all the angels with him, he will sit on his throne in heavenly glory. All the nations will be gathered before him, and he will separate the people one from another as a shepherd separates the sheep from the goats. He will put the sheep on his right and the goats on his left. Then the King will say to those on his right, 'Come, you who are blessed by my Father; take your inheritance, the kingdom prepared for you since the creation of the world.' " John in his Revelation adds, "To him who loves us and has freed us from our sins by his blood, and has made us to be a kingdom and priests to serve his God and Father — to him be glory and power for ever and ever! Amen."

To belong to Jesus means we now have a new purpose in life. The Hebrews' new purpose was to serve as a kingdom of priests in a world that did not know about the coming Savior. Free from slavery, they were free to enjoy a life of "praise, fame and honor high above all the nations he has made." In a greater way, Jesus ransomed us so that we could enjoy a kingdom He prepared for us before He created the world. Notice that! Before Jesus created the world, He set up a kingdom that we, who didn't even exist yet, could inherit. Jesus planned to make us part of the family business long before the family business even existed! The job is so important it is called priesthood, meaning we will be working side by side with God Himself!

That's quite a step up for former slaves to evil! The Hebrews never completely made that step up. They went wild with their freedom and ended up back in slavery to other nations. But Jesus gives us complete freedom from slavery to sin. It's as though ownership changed from a cruel taskmaster to a loving Father whose riches cannot be measured. Jesus Christ made this all possible when He died on a cross. His death broke the power of death by canceling sins that condemned us to death. Jesus sets us free from both grave and sinful flesh by creating in us a new life that will one day sprout a new and eternal body. Eternal life comes to us in stages. First we are set free from sin because Jesus has forgiven our sins. Next we are set free from the power of the devil as Jesus creates and builds faith in us while we listen to His Word. We wait only for the final stage of freedom when we are set free from bodies of flesh that are easily drawn into sin. But all the while, no matter what stage of eternal life we are in, we are free, free to be what Jesus planned for us to be before He created the universe. May we live up to that high calling for Jesus' sake.

Prayer: Lord Jesus, You have an inheritance waiting for us that we do not deserve, nor are we qualified to take it. We are not worth the ransom You paid for us because of sin that still clings to us like rust clings to sunken ships. Yet You claim us as Your own. Help us live up to that high calling. Stir Your Spirit in our hearts and minds that we will repent of sin. Dedicate us for service in Your kingdom, both now and forevermore, and put us to work in that kingdom. Amen.

Zechariah 9:9-10
Ephesians 1:17-23
John 12:12-17

24. The Second Article: God's Power Takes Care Of Me

> **THE APOSTLES' CREED — THE SECOND ARTICLE**
> I believe in Jesus Christ, His only Son, our Lord, who was conceived by the Holy Ghost, born of the Virgin Mary, suffered under Pontius Pilate, was crucified, dead, and buried; He descended into hell; the third day He rose again from the dead; He ascended into heaven, and sitteth on the right hand of God the Father Almighty; from thence He shall come to judge the quick and the dead. *What does this mean?* I believe that Jesus Christ ... has redeemed me ... that I may be His own and live under Him in His kingdom, and serve Him in everlasting righteousness, innocence, and blessedness....

Many people wonder what God is doing these days. Earthquakes, hurricanes, famines, wars, ethnic cleansing, recession, and many other evils weigh heavily on many people's minds, including many Christians. A look at the letter Paul wrote to the Christians in Galatia gives us a behind-the-scenes look at what God is doing. In the opening lines of his letter, Paul offers these words of encouragement: "I pray also that the eyes of your heart may be enlightened in order that you may know the hope to which he has called you, the riches of his glorious inheritance in the saints, and his incomparably great power for us who believe." I would like to focus on the last of those three blessings, "his incomparably great power for us who believe."

When Paul speaks of power, he is talking about the ability to get things done. Electrical power toasts bread and lights rooms.

Nuclear power creates the electricity. Paul speaks of God's "incomparably great power for us who believe." It is as though God is the power that makes all things possible. That power is used for Christians. I discovered how in the words that follow in Paul's letter. First, Jesus Christ has this power. Second, Jesus is the one who uses this power to take care of us in a miraculous manner.

Jesus governs with God's power. Paul writes, "That power is like the working of his mighty strength, which he exerted in Christ when he raised him from the dead and seated him at his right hand in the heavenly realms, far above all rule and authority, power and dominion, and every title that can be given, not only in the present age but also in the one to come." Take what all the most powerful people or angels can do. Jesus is able to do more. Jesus sits at the right hand of the Father. That is the Bible's way of saying that Jesus is as powerful as God the Father. How powerful is God the Father? Paul says, "that power is like the working of his mighty strength, which he exerted in Christ when he raised him from the dead and seated him at his right hand in the heavenly realms." The same power that God used to raise Jesus back to life is the power Jesus has now that he sits at the Father's right hand. That means that when God wants something done, He turns to Jesus, who carries it out with the same ability God could use to do the job. For example, Jesus is busy right now holding the atoms together that make up your body, mine, as well as all the other things of the whole creation.

Jesus takes care of his church. Paul reminds us what Jesus is doing with all that ability. "And God placed all things under his feet and appointed him to be head over everything for the church, which is his body, the fullness of him who fills everything in every way." In the same way we use every ability we have to take care of ourselves, Jesus uses His abilities to take care of the Christian church, which He treats as though it were His own flesh and blood. So, all good things are from Jesus to bless us who belong to His church.

But on the other hand, no evil happens to us that Jesus won't use it to bless us as well. Nothing happens to the church that doesn't bless it. Another way of saying that is that everything that happens blesses the church. Take the war fought in the Persian Gulf. No matter what your political beliefs are about who was right and who was wrong, and no matter who you may think won the war, consider a couple of facts. Before the war, no Christian missionaries were allowed into Saudi Arabia. But suddenly, by invitation of his royal highness the king of Saudi Arabia, thousands of Christian missionaries moved in. Sure, they were dressed in desert camouflage, but Christian soldiers and chaplains left the gospel of Jesus all over that country. Consider also the witness Christian soldiers were able to give to men and women facing danger and death in that land, a witness that would not have been as powerful if given back here in the States. The church of Jesus won that war, as it wins every war.

Jesus is no ordinary king. He is God, who set in motion plans to rescue us from this evil world long before this world existed. He is God, who manages everything that happens so that our life under Him will be blessed, both now and forever. What we do for Jesus Christ we do because He makes it possible. We can now serve Jesus in "everlasting righteousness, innocence, and blessedness."

Prayer: Jesus Christ, King of kings and Lord of lords, Master of history and Ruler of the universe: Hosanna in the highest! Words cannot tell what we owe You for all that You have given us and done for us. All we can do is ask that You would help us live lives worthy of such blessing. When times are good, help us be thankful. When times are bad, help us look past them in faith to wait for the blessings sure to follow. Give us greater faith to live free from fear of what seems to be going on around us. Inspire us with the hope You have given us, so that we will draw others into Your circle of friends and citizens. Amen.

Acts 10:34-43
Colossians 3:1-4
John 20:1-20

25. The Second Article: Risen From The Dead

> THE APOSTLES' CREED — THE SECOND ARTICLE
> I believe in Jesus Christ, His only Son, our Lord, who was conceived by the Holy Ghost, born of the Virgin Mary, suffered under Pontius Pilate, was crucified, dead, and buried; He descended into hell; the third day He rose again from the dead; He ascended into heaven, and sitteth on the right hand of God the Father Almighty; from thence He shall come to judge the quick and the dead. *What does this mean?* I believe that Jesus Christ ... has redeemed me ... even as He is risen from the dead....

Notice: believing that Jesus redeemed me is connected with believing that Jesus rose from the dead. How do I know that Jesus rose from the dead? How do I know that Abraham Lincoln was the sixteenth President of the United States? I have only written records. The people who wrote them claimed they knew Lincoln personally in some way or another. How can I know that they are telling the truth? You see, I have a collection of books about the Lone Ranger. Was there such a person? No. The records authenticate themselves. For one thing, many different documents exist about Abraham Lincoln, including some written by people who hated him. While we do sort through some tall tales about Lincoln, we have a generally good idea of who he was from what has been written about him by eyewitnesses.

This is the argument the Apostle Peter used when telling a Roman army captain named Cornelius about Jesus. "You know the message God sent to the people of Israel, telling the good news of

119

peace through Jesus Christ, who is Lord of all. You know what has happened throughout Judea, beginning in Galilee after the baptism that John preached — how God anointed Jesus of Nazareth with the Holy Spirit and power, and how he went around doing good and healing all who were under the power of the devil, because God was with him."

Peter knew that Cornelius would do what any good army commander should do — keep in touch with what is going on in the area under his command. Peter knew that Cornelius would have kept on top of the commotion Jesus had caused.

Peter adds, "What you heard about, I saw with my own eyes." "We are witnesses of everything he did in the country of the Jews and in Jerusalem. They killed him by hanging him on a tree, but God raised him from the dead on the third day and caused him to be seen. He was not seen by all the people, but by witnesses whom God had already chosen — by us who ate and drank with him after he rose from the dead. He commanded us to preach to the people and to testify that he is the one whom God appointed as judge of the living and the dead."

Peter set a pattern that will be followed through the rest of history. Already in the days of the early church, Jesus used the testimony of eyewitnesses to spread the good news of His resurrection. That's because Jesus has chosen to reveal Himself only through witnesses, not in person. Witnesses testify either what they saw or what they know.

Men like Peter left us written records of what they saw. Can we trust what they say? We know from independent sources that these men were willing to die horrible deaths rather than change their stories. Would you be willing to die for the Easter Bunny or the Lone Ranger? Either the apostles were fools, or they were liars, or they were telling the truth. If they saw Jesus alive after He was brutally murdered, then nothing else these men have to say about Jesus should be hard to believe. Why would they risk their testimony about the resurrection of Jesus by adding tall tales about Jesus walking on water or doing other miracles? They wouldn't. That especially includes what they heard Jesus say, "I have come to give my life as a ransom for many." If I can believe that Jesus rose from the dead, I can believe that I am redeemed from sin, death, and the power of the devil. You can also.

Prayer: We thank You, Holy Spirit, for preserving for us records of what God has done for us in and through Jesus Christ. Give us greater faith in these records as found in the Holy Scriptures so that we may grow in faith and hope while living in this evil world. Help us get to know the full blessings of Jesus' resurrection from the dead so that we may boldly proclaim what we know to those around us who live without that same hope. Amen.

Object lesson: What stages does a butterfly go through? Caterpillar, cocoon, butterfly. How is the butterfly different than the caterpillar? It looks different and acts different. What holiday do Christians celebrate today? Easter, when Jesus woke up from the dead after He was buried for three days. How was Jesus different after He came back from the dead? He no longer was stuck on earth in a body that could die, but lives and rules in heaven forever.

Jesus, then, is like a butterfly. He started out poor and hated by everyone. He died and was covered up. But then He came back to life, a different man!

Since Jesus rose from the dead, He promised to do the same to us. How shall we be different than we are now? We will live forever with Jesus, never to die again, or get sick or get in trouble.

The butterfly is a reminder of all this. Right now we are like the caterpillar. Someday we shall die, which is like the caterpillar being wrapped up in His cocoon. But then, like Jesus, we shall come out of our grave a new person, more beautiful than we are now, as much as a butterfly is more beautiful than a caterpillar.

Isaiah 66:10-16
1 Peter 1:3-9
Luke 22:66-71

26. The Second Article: What Jesus Does For Us Today

> **THE APOSTLES' CREED — THE SECOND ARTICLE**
> I believe in Jesus Christ, His only Son, our Lord, who was conceived by the Holy Ghost, born of the Virgin Mary, suffered under Pontius Pilate, was crucified, dead, and buried; He descended into hell; the third day He rose again from the dead; He ascended into heaven, and sitteth on the right hand of God the Father Almighty; from thence He shall come to judge the quick and the dead. *What does this mean?* I believe that Jesus Christ ... lives and reigns to all eternity.

What does it mean that Jesus lives and reigns to all eternity? To answer that, ask, "What is the job of a king?" In the Bible, a king was someone his people looked up to for care and protection. The king was the man who kept them safe from their enemies and acted as a father to the people. The reign of a king included heading up the army, being chief justice of the courts and managing the behavior of citizens so that everyone in his kingdom shared peace.

So, what is Jesus doing for us today? I find it hard to imagine what it must be like to be nearly 2000 years old. What does a guy do for 2000 years? If the job of a king is to make sure his people have safety and justice, then Jesus has been very busy. The devil, the world around us, and even the sinful human nature of Christians are enemies hell-bent on destroying our faith in Jesus and taking away our place in heaven. So Jesus has the main job of making sure we survive this evil world. He also wants to make this life worth living.

We gather today to remember how Jesus uses the power that woke Him from the dead to take care of us in this evil world. The Apostle Peter writes, "In his great mercy he has given us new birth into a living hope through the resurrection of Jesus Christ from the dead, and into an inheritance that can never perish, spoil or fade — kept in heaven for you, who through faith are shielded by God's power until the coming of the salvation that is ready to be revealed in the last time." The resurrection of Jesus demonstrates the power that God uses to keep us safe until we take over the inheritance that waits us in heaven.

But what about all the things that go wrong? How come Jesus doesn't fix them? Trouble serves a good purpose in the plan of King Jesus for us, as Saint Peter writes: "In this you greatly rejoice, though now for a little while you may have had to suffer grief in all kinds of trials. These have come so that your faith — of greater worth than gold, which perishes even though refined by fire — may be proved genuine and may result in praise, glory and honor when Jesus Christ is revealed." These words remind us that evil is under the control of King Jesus, who makes sure that anything that happens to us makes us better than before. Gold wears out, yet we still spend a lot of time purifying it. Faith, being more precious, is something Jesus spends a lot of careful attention making pure. To understand how Jesus uses what happens to us in this life to bless us, consider two stories.

A boy's toy boat went out of reach on a pond one day and started floating away. A man on the side started throwing rocks at the boat and the boy became horrified at what might happen. But then he realized that the rocks were going over the boat and making ripples that finally pushed the boat back to shore and into the boy's hands. Many times, when we stray away from God, it appears that He is throwing rocks at us. But He is really using the ripples to bring us back home.

A Persian legend tells us that a certain king needed a faithful servant and had to choose between two candidates for the office. He took both at fixed wages and told them to fill a basket with water from a nearby well, saying that he would come in the evening to inspect their work. After dumping one or two buckets of water into the basket, one of the men said, "What is the good of doing this useless work? As soon as we pour the water in, it runs out the sides." The other answered, "But we have our wages, haven't we? The use is the master's business, not ours." "I'm not going to do such fool's work," replied the complainer. Throwing down his bucket, he went away. The other man continued until he had drained the well. Looking down into it, he saw something shining at the bottom that proved to be a diamond ring. "Now I see the use of pouring water into the basket!" he exclaimed. "If the bucket had brought up the ring before the well was dry, it would have been found in the basket. Our work was not useless."

Our King Jesus makes sure that evil brings us closer to Him. He also uses the seemingly meaningless routines and drudgery of life to prepare us for glorious work in His eternal kingdom.

Prayer: Help us, Lord Jesus, to trust You more than ever before. Help us believe that the power that raised You from the dead is the same power that You use to take care of us. When times are bad, help us believe that You are drawing us closer to You. When life seems meaningless, help us believe that You are getting us ready for a purpose beyond our wildest imagination. Give us greater faith by using the preaching we hear and the sacraments we receive, according to Your promise. For You live and reign, with God the Father and the Holy Spirit, one God, now and forever. Amen.

Isaiah 61:1-3
2 Thessalonians 2:13-17
Mark 13:5-11

27. The Third Article: Called By The Gospel

> **THE APOSTLES' CREED — THE THIRD ARTICLE**
> I believe in the Holy Ghost; the holy Christian Church, the communion of saints; the forgiveness of sins; the resurrection of the body; and the life everlasting. Amen. *What does this mean?* I believe that I cannot by my own reason or strength believe in Jesus Christ, my Lord, or come to Him; but the Holy Ghost has called me by the Gospel....

How does a person become a Christian? Does a person become a Christian because he wants to? Or does a person become a Christian because God wants him to? Some people believe that a person becomes a Christian by making a personal decision. They think that faith is an act of the will, and they think that the will is informed by the mind. Thus, some people believe that a person becomes a Christian because they decided to ask Jesus into their hearts.

This is not what the Bible teaches. The Bible clearly teaches that we are Christians because God wanted us to be Christians. Listen again to what the Apostle Paul wrote to the church of the Thessalonians: "But we ought always to thank God for you, brothers loved by the Lord, because from the beginning God chose you to be saved through the sanctifying work of the Spirit and through belief in the truth. He called you to this through our gospel, that you might share in the glory of our Lord Jesus Christ." How did I become a Christian? The Bible tells me that God chose me and then He let me know when He called me by the gospel.

Imagine an orphanage filled with children of all ages and kinds. But no one wanted these children, so they are stuck in the orphanage. Then one day, the supervisor of the orphanage comes into the room full of children. "A rich man called me up and asked me if I had any children who wanted to be adopted. He told me that he has a big house with many rooms. He said that he had lots of nice clothes and good food. I told him that we had lots of children who wanted to be adopted, who didn't want to live here anymore. He told me to send them all to him. So, let's all get ready to go and meet your new daddy."

The rich man chose every one of those children. Nothing special about the children helped him make a choice except that they didn't have a home of their own. There wasn't anything any of those children did that earned them notice. They didn't decide that they wanted the rich man to take them into his family. He decided. He then sent a messenger to tell them of his choice. The supervisor merely had to collect all those the rich man chose.

"I cannot by my own reason or strength believe in Jesus Christ, my Lord, or come to Him; but the Holy Ghost has called me by the Gospel." Isaiah preached that Jesus is the one who brought the good news that heals the sick and sets the captive free. Jesus tells us that the Holy Spirit carries on the work of calling people by the gospel. He does it through the gospel proclaimed by the apostles Jesus chose: "And the gospel must first be preached to all nations. Whenever you are arrested and brought to trial, do not worry beforehand about what to say. Just say whatever is given you at the time, for it is not you speaking, but the Holy Spirit."

The Holy Spirit gave the apostles the words to say. Their preaching made the choice of God known. Today, the choice of God is made known wherever the record of the prophets and apostles is proclaimed. As that choice is proclaimed, the Holy Spirit invites people to come home to the heavenly Father.

Prayer: Heavenly Father, who has sent Your Holy Spirit to call us home to You by the preaching of the gospel about Jesus Christ, help us be a bigger part of taking that good news to others around us so that they can join us in Your family. Give us faith to support the work of those feet which bring good news with our time and our dollars. Fill us with Your Spirit through Your Word and the sacraments Jesus gave us so that we will be drawn ever closer to You. Amen.

Object lesson: (Have children gather at baptismal font. Needed: large pad of paper, marker pen. Write across top: First Name, Middle Name, Last Name.)

1. Write each child's first name in that column and their last name in the "middle name" column. Pretend to ignore any attempts to correct this.

2. Talk about what a last name means: it marks one as belonging to a family; one gets it when he is born or adopted. No one becomes a member of a family because he decides to.

3. Write "Christian" under "last name" for all the children. "Everyone here has the same last name: Christian. We were given that name when we were born again. When was that? Baptism, for most of us! We were baptized into the name of the Father and of the Son and of the Holy Spirit. We now belong to the family of God."

4. "How many brothers and sisters do we have? As many as there are Christians!"

Psalm 119:105-112
1 Peter 2:4-9
John 1:1-13

28. The Third Article: Enlightened With His Gifts

> THE APOSTLES' CREED — THE THIRD ARTICLE
> I believe in the Holy Ghost; the holy Christian Church, the communion of saints; the forgiveness of sins; the resurrection of the body; and the life everlasting. Amen. *What does this mean?* I believe that ... the Holy Ghost has ... enlightened me with His gifts....

In the letter to the Hebrews we read, "Therefore, brothers, since we have boldness for the way of entry into the holy place by the blood of Jesus, which he inaugurated for us as a new and living way through the curtain, that is, his flesh, and since we have a great high priest over the house of God, let us approach with true hearts in the full assurance of faith, having had our hearts sprinkled from a wicked conscience and our bodies bathed with clean water. Let us hold fast the public declaration of our hope without wavering, for he is faithful that promised. And let us consider one another to incite to love and fine works, not forsaking the gathering of ourselves together, as some have the custom, but encouraging one another, and all the more so as you behold the day drawing near." Notice that these words point out two main truths. First, Jesus makes it possible for us to worship and serve God. Second, we should gather in public often and regularly to remind each other of our hope in Christ and our duties toward Him.

How many of you know that God always says "yes" to the prayers of Christians? How many of you know why Hebrew baby boys were circumcised and why no similar ceremony existed for girls? Why did Jesus preach in parables? What difference did it make whether the priests used incense or not before entering into the inner room of the Temple? Why does God seem so bloodthirsty in the Old Testament but so kind and gentle in the New Testament? I have hundreds of other questions I could ask you, but they all have one thing in common: how well do you know Jesus? The better you know Jesus, the more you will want to do things for Him. That's always true for us. The better we know anyone, the more we will be ready to do things for him.

The Scriptures are a lamp to our feet and a light to our path. That's because the whole Bible is about Jesus, who is the light that has come into the world to give light to people. Think of a flashlight. Jesus is the glow, the Bible is the case. Anyone who has a flashlight can see in the dark where to go. Anyone who has a Bible can see where to go in life, because Jesus reveals the path. He is the light of the world, as John tells us in his Gospel about the days after the arrival of John the baptizer: "The true light that gives light to every sort of man was about to come into the world ... and the world came into existence through him, but the world did not know him. He came to his own home, but his own people did not take him in. However, as many as did receive him, to them he gave authority to become God's children, because they were exercising faith in his name; and they were born, not from blood or from a fleshly will or from man's will, but from God." John spends the rest of his Gospel telling us that Jesus Christ was that light.

The next time you drive down the highway some moonless night, try a little experiment. Turn off your headlights. Then drive the rest of the way home. On second thought, that is a stupid idea. Don't do it. You could get hurt! The same is true about Jesus. Who would be so foolish that he would turn Jesus off and then try to find his way through life to his heavenly home? As silly as that idea sounds, that is what happens when Christians avoid hearing about Jesus as often as they can. Saint Peter tells us, "We have the prophetic word made more sure; and you are doing well in paying attention to it as to a lamp shining in a dark place, until day dawns and a daystar rises, in your hearts. For you know this first, that no prophecy of Scripture springs from any private interpretation. For prophecy was at no time brought by man's will, but men spoke from God as they were borne along by Holy Spirit." The Bible clearly teaches that one of the jobs the Spirit of God has is to shine light into our lives by what is written in the Bible.

Is God's Word part of your daily routine? You don't have to go to church every day, though if at all possible, you should get together with other Christians as often as possible. Most of you have at least two Bibles in your homes. When it is not practicable to gather with other Christians in church, you still can gather with the saints of all times by spending time studying the Bible. And it makes no difference what version you use. All the verses I quoted in this message came from the Bible used by the Jehovah's Witnesses! All translations suffer in some degree from mistranslation. Sometimes, beliefs color how a translator translates difficult words or sentences. The light might be dimmed somewhat by the sinfulness of people who translate the Bible, but Jesus still shines through to those He has called. Such is the power of God's Spirit. Humble pen and ink, like humble water or humble bread and wine, are used by God's Spirit as wrappings in which He offers Jesus to us. These gifts are what "enlighten us."

Prayer: Holy Spirit, who shines the light of truth into our lives through the testimony given about Jesus in the Bible, give us faith in Jesus, the light of the world. Help us be thankful for all the gifts you give us that shine the light of Jesus in our lives. Help us be thankful for the gift of Holy Scriptures, which testify to Jesus, the light of the world, as John the Baptist did. Help us be thankful for our baptism, which joined us to the death and resurrection of Jesus the light of the world. Help us be thankful for the gift of Holy Communion, which shines the forgiveness of sins into our lives from Jesus the light of the world. In many ways You have enlightened us with Your gifts so that we can stay on the path that leads to heaven. Give us greater faith to use those gifts so that we will not needlessly bump into temptation and other shame and vice. Amen.

Psalm 51:1-12
1 Peter 1:1-5
John 17:1-17

29. The Third Article: Sanctified And Kept In Faith

> THE APOSTLES' CREED — THE THIRD ARTICLE
> I believe in the Holy Ghost; the holy Christian Church, the communion of saints; the forgiveness of sins; the resurrection of the body; and the life everlasting. Amen. *What does this mean?* I believe that ... the Holy Ghost has ... sanctified and kept me in the true faith....

No matter how much a man tries to reform himself, he can never achieve the newness of life that God wants him to have in Christ. Although a man can make changes in his life, even positive changes, he still remains the same person and often goes from one kind of problem to another. Sports broadcaster Harry Kalas once introduced a Philadelphia Phillies baseball player, Garry Maddox, with the following words: "He has turned his life around. He used to be depressed and miserable. Now he's miserable and depressed."

The Bible teaches that we can achieve newness of life only one way. We need the help of the Holy Spirit. King David understood this very well. He had an affair with a woman and had her husband killed so he could marry her. But David could not escape his sin. When the whole mess became public, he threw himself on the mercy of God. David's Psalm 51 is his personal prayer to God. But this prayer is our prayer also. In this psalm we confess that we are unable to be the kind of people God wants us to be. We also confess that only God can make us the kind of people He wants us to be.

"Have mercy on me, O God, according to your unfailing love; according to your great compassion blot out my transgressions. Wash away all my iniquity and cleanse me from my sin. For I know my transgressions, and my sin is always before me. Against you,

you only, have I sinned and done what is evil in your sight, so that you are proved right when you speak and justified when you judge. Surely I was sinful at birth, sinful from the time my mother conceived me." Some of these words have hit me the hardest: "Against you, you only, have I sinned and done what is evil in your sight." What about the man David killed? What about the people we sin against? Don't they count? Of course they do! We sin against God alone because we do sin against each other. When we gossip, or spit out angry words, or insult or hurt other people in any other way, we might as well pound a nail into the hand of Jesus.

Why do I say that? Try an experiment the next time you visit someone's home. First, start moving the furniture around in the living room. When you finish eating, turn to someone in your family and say, "This tasted pretty bad. I could do better blindfolded." As you leave, take a walk through the flower bed in front of the house. Then see how long it is before you are invited back. My guess is that your hosts will be offended, though you never once said or did anything to them. That's because when we insult the handiwork of a person, we insult the person. Likewise, when we sin against each other, we are really sinning against the God who created each of us and who shed His blood for each of us. We are His handiwork.

David shows us in his prayer how God takes away that sin. "Cleanse me with hyssop, and I will be clean; wash me, and I will be whiter than snow." That makes me think of baptism right away. Hyssop was what folks used as a scouring pad in those days. We ask God to scour us clean, and in Jesus' name, baptism does just that.

"Let me hear joy and gladness; let the bones you have crushed rejoice. Hide your face from my sins and blot out all my iniquity." These words make me think of the good news preached about Jesus. Shepherds used to break the legs of wandering sheep. This meant that the shepherd would have to feed the sheep personally. Soon the sheep would learn to love and trust the shepherd. I know that sorrow is meant to drive me closer to Jesus. I can rejoice because now I know that Jesus has forgiven me the sins that earn me eternal punishment.

"Create in me a pure heart, O God, and renew a steadfast spirit within me. Do not cast me from your presence or take your Holy Spirit from me." These are the words that teach us how God plans to change us. First, He must give us a new heart. The heart stands for the person's whole life. What comes out of a person's heart goes all through his body. Jesus tells us that it is from the heart whence all evil springs. God must give us a new heart, a new personality. We also need a spirit that will stand up to temptation. The normal human spirit is not strong enough to endure temptation. That new heart and steadfast spirit is given to us at our baptism, when we are joined to Jesus. We pray that God would stay with us. We especially pray that God would not take His Holy Spirit from us. If you wonder what would happen if God were to take his Spirit from us, all you have to do is remember what happens when He takes our spirit from us — we die. His Spirit gives us eternal life, so if that is gone, we are dead forever.

We cannot hope to be holy unless God stays close to us. God does this as His Word is preached and the sacraments Jesus gave us are used. Jesus prayed for His disciples, "Father, make them holy by the truth. Your word is truth." He also told His disciples that He was giving them the gift of the Holy Spirit to help them. We don't need self-help books to be better. We need the Holy Spirit opening up our hearts and minds to what God says. It does not matter that we cannot remember all we hear. Maybe your mind is like a sieve, everything leaks through. When you pour water over a sieve, no matter how much you pour, you don't collect much. But at least you end up with a clean sieve. God's Word will do better than water on a sieve. We can also take comfort in knowing that the day is coming when we will not be sieves anymore.

Prayer: Holy Spirit, Gift divine, give us greater faith than ever before as we hear about the good things Jesus has done for us so that we will be able to stand up against temptation. Forgive us for thinking that we can live holy lives without any help from You. Give us a greater love for the Bible You have given us and the sacraments that act out the same message of grace. Amen.

Psalm 85
Ephesians 4:1-16
Matthew 16:13-19

30. The Third Article: He Calls, Gathers, Enlightens The Whole Church

> **THE APOSTLES' CREED — THE THIRD ARTICLE**
> I believe in the Holy Ghost; the holy Christian Church, the communion of saints; the forgiveness of sins; the resurrection of the body; and the life everlasting. Amen. *What does this mean?* I believe that ... the Holy Ghost ... calls, gathers, enlightens, and sanctifies the whole Christian Church on earth....

"I don't have to go to church to be a Christian." Ever heard anyone say that? Ever thought it yourself? I have. And the truth of the matter is, you *don't* have to go to church to be a Christian. Otherwise people who are shut up in their own homes or in nursing homes couldn't be Christians. If you had to go to church to be a Christian, what happens to you on Monday through Saturday when you aren't in church?

So, what good is going to church? Or, what good is having the church come to you when you are sick in the hospital or a nursing home or your own home? What difference does it make to have a bunch of people get together, call a pastor, and meet once or more a week to worship Jesus in public? Couldn't they worship Jesus in private? Couldn't they study their Bibles in private? Do you really need a pastor to do baptisms or serve Holy Communion or teach the Bible in order to be a Christian?

The Bible is clear about what it takes to be a Christian: "Whoever calls on the name of the Lord Jesus will be saved." "Faith comes by hearing and hearing by what is preached about Christ." "Whoever believes and is baptized shall be saved."

The great man of faith in the Bible, Abraham, never went to church. There weren't any in his day. But he was a man of God who trusted in God to forgive his sins and take him to an eternal home.

So why do we have churches? For much the same reason as we have places to take our cars when we need gasoline or repairs. Couldn't you take care of your car at home? Some people do have their own tools and gas storage tanks. Why don't we all? And why do those who have their own tools and shops and gas storage tanks still come to the service station? Isn't it because service stations make the job of taking care of your car easier? The professional mechanics probably can fix cars faster than you can at home. And those of you who can't fix cars, either because you never have had the time to learn how, or because you are as mechanically inclined as a grapefruit, you can hardly get along without the service station! The point is, we don't need service stations to take care of our cars, and yet wherever you find cars, you find service stations.

The church is like a service station. The Apostle Paul describes this in his letter to the church of Ephesus. "It was he who gave some to be apostles, some to be prophets, some to be evangelists, and some to be pastors and teachers, to prepare God's people for works of service, so that the body of Christ may be built up until we all reach unity in the faith and in the knowledge of the Son of God and become mature, attaining to the whole measure of the fullness of Christ." Churches are where you find prophets and apostles and evangelists and pastors and teachers doing the work of preparing God's people for works of service and helping them grow up in faith.

If you didn't have a church to go to or a church that is taking care of you, you probably also don't have a pastor. Pastors are like the professional car mechanics. Pastors know a lot of shortcuts when it comes to studying God's Word. They have spent many, many hours at the feet of prophets, apostles, and evangelists getting to know Jesus in the Bible. Pastors are especially equipped to show you all the blessings Jesus has in store for you in His Word and sacraments. Paul tells us that pastors are one of the gifts Jesus gives to the church to help us grow up in our faith. People without a pastor have a hard time growing up.

Churches are also a blessing for people who can't or won't come to church. Church members pool their resources so they can pay a man to use his training to make house calls and train others to do this work. So the pastor and his helpers take the good news of Jesus to those in the hospital, in the nursing home, and those who are too sick to come to church. He also represents Jesus in the homes of people who won't come to church. The rest of the congregation prays that members who can't come to church will be reminded of the love of Jesus and those who have fallen away would then be drawn back into the support circle of the church by the love of Jesus.

We would find it hard to remain Christian without our church. If you don't believe that, consider the history of God's people before Jesus. Until only a few hundred years before Jesus, God's people did not go to church. Church, as we know it, was not invented until after the Temple was destroyed and the people were carried off to Babylon. Before that, only the men were required to travel to God's house, and only three times a year. Thus, the people did not get much exposure to God's Word. And look how wicked they were, including so-called heroes of faith like Samson, David and others like them. Furthermore, consider those who have dropped out of church. The longer they stay away from the church, the harder it is to tell them apart from those who never went to church!

What an extra blessing we have today because we have a church to belong to! The Holy Spirit uses the church as a center of spiritual nurture and care where he can unfold the Word of God in all of its blessings to us. The church is where the good news of Jesus is clearly taught and faith built in ways that are difficult without the church and its pastors. May we not take this blessing for granted.

Prayer: Holy Spirit, Giver of life, who spoke by the prophets and helps keep God's people with Jesus, bless our church with pure preaching and teaching. Help our pastor show the love of Jesus in what he says and what he does. Help us all grow up under the leadership of this pastor which You and Jesus gave us as a royal gift of love. Forgive us for the times we have neglected gathering in this place to hear about Jesus. And be with those who cannot be here with us by inspiring us to go and be with them, taking the good news of Jesus with us as we go. Amen.

Jeremiah 31:31-34
Ephesians 1:1-14
Matthew 18:15-22

31. The Third Article: Rich And Daily Forgiveness

> **THE APOSTLES' CREED — THE THIRD ARTICLE**
> I believe in the Holy Ghost; the holy Christian Church, the communion of saints; the forgiveness of sins; the resurrection of the body; and the life everlasting. Amen. *What does this mean?* I believe that ... the Holy Ghost ... [in the Christian Church] daily and richly forgives all sins to me and all believers....

Why do churches exist? I think most people agree that churches exist to do something about wickedness. But, unfortunately, three main ideas exist about how churches should treat wickedness. A large number of churches think that the job of the church is to use political force to get rid of wickedness. They think all we have to do is pass laws and enforce them and we can get rid of poverty, crime, and violence. Other churches think that all they have to do to get rid of wickedness is to teach people how to live holy lives. Those kinds of churches are well known for all the rules they have about how to dress, how to act in public, what is forbidden. Both these groups have similar ideas. They share the common belief that if we change people's behavior, we will get rid of wickedness. We, however, believe that the church gets rid of wickedness by forgiving it.

One day, Jesus' disciples asked him who was the greatest in the kingdom of heaven. His answer came in two parts. First, whoever takes good spiritual care of children is great in God's kingdom. Jesus then went on to describe another way to be great in the kingdom of heaven: forgive sins, especially of fellow Christians.

Jesus gave this as the work of the church. Jesus said, "If your brother sins against you, go and show him his fault, just between the two of you. If he listens to you, you have won your brother over. But if he will not listen, take one or two others along, so that 'every matter may be established by the testimony of two or three witnesses.' If he refuses to listen to them, tell it to the church; and if he refuses to listen even to the church, treat him as you would a pagan or a tax collector." Notice that the church is the final court in settling a dispute between Christians.

Jesus explains why this should be this way when he went on to say, "I tell you the truth, whatever you bind on earth will be bound in heaven, and whatever you loose on earth will be loosed in heaven." This is the main principle of forgiveness. A church court can forgive or not forgive sins because Jesus has given the church the job of doing this on behalf of heaven itself.

Jesus then tells us what makes up a church when he said, "Again, I tell you that if two of you on earth agree about anything you ask for, it will be done for you by my Father in heaven. For where two or three come together in my name, there am I with them." The name Jesus is the name by which all people are saved. Therefore, to gather in Jesus' name is to gather for the purpose of saving people. Jesus gave us two main ways to do this, by baptizing people, which washes away their sins, and by teaching them about forgiveness. He gave us two different ways to teach. We can proclaim the good news with words about how Jesus' death won us forgiveness, or, as Saint Paul pointed out in a letter to the Corinthians, we proclaim the death of Jesus each time we eat his body and drink his blood in Holy Communion, a meal Jesus left us that offers forgiveness of sin. So, a church can be known by one thing: are Christians handing out forgiveness when they gather together?

A true Christian church does not make holiness demands on its members before allowing them to enjoy the blessings of fellowship with Jesus. Instead, a true Christian church will seek out the wicked and work to absorb them. That's why, in our church, we let only sinners join. Remember, we all have to stand up in front of everybody at one time or another and admit that we are sinners before we can be a full communicant member! No sin is too bad, no shame too great that people cannot bring them here and have them forgiven. For it is in the church that the Holy Spirit "richly and daily forgives sins to me and all believers." As we are forgiven, the Spirit goes to work creating a new heart in us so that we can live forgiven lives. That is the promise God made in His new covenant.

Prayer: Holy Spirit of God, the Lord and the One who gives life, we thank You for the miracle of grace You work in our midst as You use the Word and sacraments of Jesus to forgive our sins and create new hearts in us. Forgive us if we ever think of our church as a club for nice people. Help us remember that we exist as a church to seek the sinners who live around us and gather them in with us to taste of the many-sided forgiveness Jesus won for us in His death and resurrection. Bless us when we reach out with that good news and prod us into action if we get lazy and indifferent. Amen.

Isaiah 42:1-7
1 Corinthians 15:20-26
John 6:32-44

32. The Third Article: Raise Up Me And All The Dead

> **THE APOSTLES' CREED — THE THIRD ARTICLE**
> I believe in the Holy Ghost; the holy Christian Church, the communion of saints; the forgiveness of sins; the resurrection of the body; and the life everlasting. Amen. *What does this mean?* I believe that ... the Holy Ghost ... will at the Last Day raise up me and all the dead....

Many years ago, the ship known as the *Empress of Ireland* went down with 130 Salvation Army officers on board, along with many other passengers. Only 21 of those Christian workers' lives were spared — an unusually small number. Why? Of the 109 workers who drowned, not one body had on a life preserver! Many of the survivors told how those brave people, seeing that there were not enough lifebelts, took off their own and strapped them onto others, saying, "I know Jesus, so I can die better than you can."

Why does knowing Jesus help us die better? Think of the last cliffhanger adventure you either saw or read. The hero goes from one life-threatening mess to the next. If he gets caught in the bad guy's trap, or gets seriously injured, we feel bad, but we don't give up. We know that the hero will somehow pull through. In a much bigger way, we don't fear death or anything that leads up to it because we know how the story is going to end up. And if we see that cliffhanger again, we know for sure how it will end up!

In a bigger way, we know how the story will end up for us after we die. "Christ has indeed been raised from the dead, the firstfruits of those who have fallen asleep. For since death came through a man, the resurrection of the dead comes also through a man. For as in Adam all die, so in Christ all will be made alive. But each in his own turn: Christ, the firstfruits; then, when he comes, those who belong to him." Since we believe that Jesus Christ rose from the dead, it is easy for us to believe that He will also wake us from the dead.

Many different funeral directors have told me that church funerals are easier to do than non-church funerals. And they have told me that funerals of active church members are easier than of non-active members. That's because the closer the dead person was to Jesus, the less the family grieves or is tormented by the death of that person. If the family has hope to see their loved one again, the tears are not so bitter, the cries are not so anguished. Instead, the tears are like those shed when friends move away, but we still hope to see them again.

This hope is a gift of the Holy Spirit, part of the faith He creates in us as we learn about Jesus. Not only so, but we know that the same Holy Spirit who raised Jesus to life will raise us also. It is as Paul writes in his letter to the Romans, "And if the Spirit of him who raised Jesus from the dead is living in you, he who raised Christ from the dead will also give life to your mortal bodies through his Spirit, who lives in you."

Think of it as divine CPR. Someone collapses from a heart attack, or drowns. What are we supposed to do? First we start breathing into him, right? Without breath, all the heart pumping and drugs in the world will do nothing to bring the person back. And if we don't get to the person within a few minutes, the lack of breath will quickly kill delicate organs like the brain and kidneys. But if we can get breath into the person quickly, we have a good chance of reviving him.

On the Last Day a greater miracle will take place. God has a breath that revives a body that has completely dissolved in the grave or by fire or water. The Bible calls that breath the Holy Spirit. It is this living breath of God that stirred life from nothing back at the dawn of time. This is the Spirit the Lord Jesus has already breathed into us. For most of us, that happened at our baptism, when "the renewal of the Holy Spirit was poured out on us." So it's only a matter of time before we wake from the dead!

Prayer: Holy Spirit, Giver of life, continue to breathe into us the life that will carry us from this life into the next. If we should die before the Last Day, keep our bodies safe in the certain hope of the resurrection of the dead. Comfort us with this hope as we face the loss of loved ones who know Jesus. And for those who don't know Jesus, give us the courage to tell them about Jesus and the hope He gives to us since He has revived from the dead and lives eternally on high with You and the Father, ever one God, world without end. Amen.

Object lesson: What happens when we bury a seed? It changes and grows into a plant. What will a corn seed grow into? A corn plant. What is different between the seed and the plant that grows from it? The plant is much bigger. The plant looks different than the seed, usually much more beautiful. Yet there is still something the same about the plant: it has seeds in it.

How many of you know someone who has died? What happened to the body? It was buried, just as we bury seeds.

Do you know what the Bible promises will happen to those who are buried, who believed in Jesus before they died? The Bible promises that, like a seed planted in the ground, after we die our human bodies will grow into new bodies that will still be human, but much better and more beautiful than what we have now.

"God so loved the world that he gave his only begotten Son, that whoever believes in him shall not perish, but have eternal life," (John 3:16).

Joel 3:9-21
Galatians 6:1-8
John 3:13-21

33. The Third Article: God's Gift Of Eternal Life

> THE APOSTLES' CREED — THE THIRD ARTICLE
> I believe in the Holy Ghost; the holy Christian Church, the communion of saints; the forgiveness of sins; the resurrection of the body; and the life everlasting. Amen. *What does this mean?* I believe that ... the Holy Ghost ... will at the Last Day ... give unto me and all believers in Christ eternal life.

The Apostle Paul wrote to the church in Galatia, "Do not be deceived: God cannot be mocked. A man reaps what he sows. The one who sows to please his sinful nature, from that nature will reap destruction; the one who sows to please the Spirit, from the Spirit will reap eternal life." On this the last Sunday of the Epiphany season, let us pause and think about the future. The Bible talks about a day of harvest coming, a harvest of souls. Two kinds of Christians will be at that harvest.

On the day of judgment, there will be some who claim to be Christians who will be turned away from God's kingdom. Jesus told us that many would say, "Lord, Lord, didn't we do this and that and the other thing in your name," and He will say, "Go away, I don't know you." These false Christians will be like counterfeit money when it reaches the bank.

Suppose you are given a counterfeit ten-dollar bill in change at the store. You pay your babysitter. Thinking it is genuine, the babysitter uses it to pay for some gas. The station owner uses it to pay one of his employees, who uses it to buy groceries. From there it goes to the bank, where the teller says, "I'm sorry, but this bill is counterfeit." The bill may have been used to do a lot of good while it was in circulation, but when it arrived at the bank, it was exposed for what it really was and put out of circulation. A counterfeit Christian may do many good works, but still be rejected at the gates of judgment.

An Indiana cemetery has a tombstone over a hundred years old that bears this epitaph: "Pause, Stranger, when you pass me by, As you are now, so once was I. As I am now, so you will be, So prepare for death and follow me." An unknown passerby had read those words and scratched this reply below them: "To follow you I'm not content Until I know which way you went." The passerby was right — the important thing about death is what follows it. Where are you going? Those who sow to the flesh will reap destruction. The Bible tells us that flesh and blood cannot inherit the kingdom of heaven.

Some examples of Christians sowing to the flesh include anger, immorality, lust, hypocrisy, lying, cheating, and all those other sins condemned in the Bible. Christians who think they can go to church on Sunday and live like heathens on Monday through Saturday are sowing to the flesh. They are as phony as a counterfeit dollar bill. Counterfeit money ends up in the fire. So do counterfeit Christians.

Jesus wants to help us sow to the Spirit. Since the Spirit is the one who creates and maintains faith in us, Jesus gives us this promise, "But whoever lives by the truth comes into the light, so that it may be seen plainly that what he has done has been done through God." The light Jesus speaks of is Himself. The truth he speaks of is the Word which the Holy Spirit has carefully given to us by prophets and apostles in the Scriptures. So all we have to do to live by the truth is get to know the Scriptures, because they tell us of Jesus. And when we live by the truth, God's way of doing things will show up in our lives.

Saint Paul, in another place, calls doing things God's way fruits of the Spirit. He lists them as love, joy, peace, long-suffering, kindness, goodness, faithfulness, gentleness, self-control. If you are like me, you have a long way to go before these fruits show up in your life the way they did in Jesus' life. Who could be more long-suffering than Jesus, who must put up with our hypocrisy and sinfulness? Who could be more gentle than Jesus, who works to create a new heart in us rather than kicking us to pieces? Who is more kind than Jesus, who turns the other cheek and rewards evil with sun that shines on the wicked and rain that falls on the unrighteous?

If these and the other fruits of the Spirit are not mature, take heart! Those who stay close to Jesus have His promise that we shall reap eternal life one day. The fruits of the Spirit may seem shriveled and tiny now, but the truth of Jesus, as a food for our souls fed us by God's Spirit, will nourish us until we reach maturity and we produce the same fruits as Jesus has. Jesus tells us that if we eat His flesh and drink his blood, we will live forever. Only faith can do this. That's why Jesus gives us the gift of the Holy Spirit. Remember, the Holy Spirit's job is to get us ready to live forever! First He gives us saving faith. Then He brings that faith to fruit.

Prayer: We thank You, Holy Spirit, that through the work done by You in the Church, You prepare us for eternal life. Help us be ready for that final day by inspiring us to get closer to the truth that points us to Jesus. Forgive us for making excuses when we avoid spending time in getting to know the Scriptures better. Forgive us for the times we have avoided gathering in church. Bless our time here with fruits of faith that make us more like Jesus. Amen.

Isaiah 63:8-16
1 John 1:1-3
Matthew 6:5-8

34. The Introduction: Our Father In Heaven

> **THE LORD'S PRAYER — THE INTRODUCTION**
> Our Father who art in heaven. *What does this mean?*
> God would by these words tenderly invite us to believe that He is our true Father, and that we are His true children, so that we may with all boldness and confidence ask Him as dear children ask their dear father.

The word "father" brings up mixed feelings among many people. Some people have good feelings. They think fondly about their fathers, like the family vacations their fathers took them on or the other fun things they remember doing with their dads. Some have bad feelings. They remember being beaten, yelled at, abused, neglected, or even abandoned. It seems risky that God would reveal Himself to us as a father. Those who have had bad fathers might be afraid of God if He is a father. And those who have had good fathers might think that if God is a father, that means always having fun with Him and having good times. When Jesus teaches us to pray, however, He tells us that God is different than any father you or I might know. Jesus said, "When you pray, pray like this, 'Our Father, who art in heaven.'" Jesus tells us that we have a heavenly Father. While it is good to know that God is our Father, the really good news is found in knowing that He is our Father in heaven.

The Lord Jesus tells us two things that are different about our heavenly Father than about earthly fathers: our heavenly Father sees what is done in secret and He knows what we need before we ask Him. Some of us had dads who had eyes in the backs of their heads. Our heavenly Father sees better than that! He sees what we do in private, behind closed doors. Some of us have had fathers who gave us gifts on our birthdays or at Christmas that were just what we wanted, but only after we begged and begged and begged for them. Our heavenly Father knows what we need before we ask Him — always, and He always gets it right. He searches our hearts with his Holy Spirit so that He knows what we need better than we know. The Father who sees what happens in secret also knows what we need before we can ask Him.

The idea that God sees what we do in secret can be scary. Many of us have done things hoping that our fathers would never find out. Yet there is a Father who sees what we do in secret. If what He sees is sin, we have reason to fear. But Jesus tells us that the heavenly Father is not snooping in on our lives to catch us doing wrong. He can't catch us doing anything wrong. That's because Jesus forgives what we do faster than we can do it. As long as we are trusting Jesus to forgive our sins, our heavenly Father will only see good and faithful children. So he is not snooping around looking for secret sin. Instead, our heavenly Father watches us closely to catch us doing something good in secret. Those bedtime prayers, those silent prayers we pray before starting a tough job, catch God's eye. He keeps track of each of them and rewards them as acts of great service. How much more can we be confident that our heavenly Father will take notice of other acts of service done in His name!

The idea that God knows what we need before we can ask might tempt us to think, "Why bother asking?" But remember, it is not the asking that gets us what we need. We are going to get what we need whether we ask for it or not. God sends sun to shine on the good and bad and rain to fall on the righteous and unrighteous. This is the Father who sent His only begotten Son Jesus into human flesh to bear our sin and be our Savior, long before we knew or cared about being saved. He didn't wait for our prayers before He would save us. Prayer, then, is something that happens after we get what we need. Asking is faith in action. When we ask somebody for something, it's because we believe he can help us and might want to. In a greater way, we can confidently ask our heavenly Father for things because He delights in being asked and enjoys watching us enjoy His answers.

When we pray, it is like a little child climbing up into the lap of his dad. Nobody else has to see that. Dad is Dad, even when no one else is around. The child doesn't have to wait until a crowd of people is around before he can say, "O Dad, please give ear unto my request and harken to my needs. Send me food and clothing and protect me from harm." The child just climbs up into Dad's lap and looks into Dad's eyes. Most children learn to trust Dad — even if Dad makes mistakes. How much more can we come before our heavenly Father trusting His goodness and love! Indeed, we can come to Him with boldness and confidence. The sky is the limit, because that is where our heavenly Father lives and works.

Prayer: Lord Jesus, help us always believe that we have a Father in heaven who pays close attention to us so that we get the good things He wants us to have. Help us love Him dearly so we can enjoy His love for us more than ever before. Amen.

Psalm 103:1-14
2 Thessalonians 1:6-12
John 17:11-17

35. The First Petition: Hallowed Be Thy Name

> **THE LORD'S PRAYER — THE FIRST PETITION**
> Hallowed be Thy name. *What does this mean?* God's name is indeed holy in itself; but we pray in this petition that it may be holy among us also. *How is this done?* When the Word of God is taught in its truth and purity, and we, as the children of God, also lead a holy life according to it. This grant us, dear Father in heaven. But he that teaches and lives otherwise than God's Word teaches, profanes the name of God among us. From this preserve us, Heavenly Father.

Ask anyone if he or she believes in God and you will usually get the answer, "Of course I believe in God." But ask what God they believe in, and they'll say, "What do you mean, which God! I believe in the Lord." Our money says, "In God We Trust." One cannot be a Boy Scout or join the Masonic lodge or other lodges unless one says he believes in God. How many times do we read in *Reader's Digest* or hear on some television news program someone say, "The Lord did this or that for me"? But that doesn't mean they are talking about the same Lord or God you and I talk about. Almost every religion uses the words "god" or "lord" as names for the supernatural being they worship. But there are many supernatural beings. "All roads lead up the same mountain," some say. "It makes no difference." Because of this, the names "God" or "Lord" are basically meaningless when we are outside the walls of our church. "God" or "Lord" are not specific enough. It's like those generic brands we see in stores — white boxes with plain black labeling that have no brand name. Yet what is in the box or can is not always from the same source.

A similar situation existed in the land of the Israelites, from the days of Moses up to a few hundred years before Christ came. Ask anyone if he believed in "the Lord," and he would say, "Of course." The word they used was a common name for supernatural beings, "Baal," which means something like our word "Lord." It's what one called a person of authority. Sarah called Abraham "her Baal." The kings were called "Baals." Even Jehovah is called "Baal" in the original language. You can imagine the confusion and irritation many people had when preachers began telling people that the Lord they worshiped was a devil. "Everybody worships the Lord. What difference does it make if we up north worship the Lord by sacrificing babies to him and sacred dances, and you down south worship him by dancing around your maypoles and spending an hour with one of the virgin priestesses?" The various Baals had other names like Marduk, El. The people even called Jehovah "Baal." Folks in those days would say something like, "A rose by any other name would smell as sweet — Baal by any other name is still God."

In the Lord's Prayer we say, "Our Father who art in heaven, hallowed be Thy name." Did you know that some Jews and other religions use this prayer in their worship? We and they all use the words "Lord" and "Father" to speak of God. So are we speaking to the same God? No. Whose name do we want to hallow? "Will the real heavenly Father please stand up!" Consider what Jesus of Nazareth once said in a prayer to God: "Holy Father, protect them by the power of your name — the name you gave me — so that they may be one as we are one." Here Jesus talks about a name that He and God the heavenly Father have in common. Jesus claimed to be God! Who can I give my name to? Only to my children. Jesus claims to be the Son of God. Paul picks up on this when he writes that God the heavenly Father gave to Jesus "the name that is above every name, that at the name of Jesus, every knee should bow in heaven, on earth and beneath the earth." Only one name is above all other names — God's name. Clearly, Jesus believed that His name was Jehovah. The apostles believed that also, because many times they quoted Old Testament Scriptures that spoke about Jehovah, and said that these were talking about Jesus. So if a person worships a God whose name is not Jesus, he is worshiping a false God. And if a person worships someone called Jesus, but his Jesus is not God over all, it is a false Jesus.

So only Christians can hallow God's name. If anyone else besides a Christian prays the Lord's Prayer, he is misusing God's name. "Hallow" means "to treat as holy or sacred." Jesus tells us how. "Sanctify them by the truth; your word is truth." "Sanctify" (a Latin word) means the same thing as "hallow" (the Old English way of saying it). First, before we can hallow or sanctify God's name, He must hallow or sanctify us! He gives us His Holy Spirit — His "Spirit of Hallowness." When God does this for us, a change takes place. We begin to believe what we need to believe. Then, we begin to behave like we ought to behave. That's because a holy person becomes like the one who is the pattern of all holiness, Jesus Christ. We were baptized into the name of the Father, Son, and Holy Spirit. That means God plans to make us like Him. And the tool He uses is, as Jesus said, His Word. "Sanctify them by the truth. Your word is truth." John tells us in his Gospel that Jesus is the Word of God made flesh. Jesus also said, "I am the way, the truth, and the life." Thus God sanctifies us, hallows us, through Jesus Christ.

That means that the only way God's name can be hallowed is, as Dr. Luther so nicely put it, "when the Word of God is taught in its truth and purity and we as the children of God also lead a holy life according to it." While it is often unpleasant to have to tell people that the lord or god they worship is a devil, or say that they do not teach God's Word in its truth and purity, to stay silent is to bring dishonor on the name of Jesus by allowing demons or their doctrines to get the same honor as Jesus. Lutherans are not "fundamentalists." Fundamentalists say that there are certain doctrines that must be believed, but that the rest are open for debate. Lutherans believe that no doctrine is open for debate because Jesus said, "Teach them all that I have taught you." We must point out false doctrine and cults and work to correct error. We must pray that God would help us keep our doctrine straight. But we must also pray that God would change our hearts so that our behavior doesn't bring dishonor to Him either. Bad behavior brings dishonor to God as much as bad doctrine. We get help for all this as we study the Scriptures and use God's sacraments.

Prayer: While we remain in this world, Holy Father, protect us by the power of Your name — the name You gave Jesus — so that we may be one as You and Jesus are one. Give us the full measure of joy Jesus wanted us to have. He gave us Your Word and the world has hated us, for we are not of the world any more than Jesus is of the world. Protect us from the Evil One because we are not of the world. Sanctify us by the truth which we find in Your Word and sacraments. Amen.

1 Samuel 8:1-9
Colossians 1:9-14
Matthew 13:24-34

36. The Second Petition: Thy Kingdom Come

> **THE LORD'S PRAYER — THE SECOND PETITION**
> Thy kingdom come. *What does this mean?* The kingdom of God comes indeed without our prayer, of itself; but we pray in this petition that it may come unto us also. *How is this done?* When our heavenly Father gives us His Holy Spirit, so that by His grace we believe His holy Word and lead a godly life, here in time and hereafter in eternity.

Christians do not all agree about how God answers the prayer, "Thy kingdom come." Some have the idea that God's kingdom comes whenever government is taken over by Christians. These people think that all we have to do is use the Bible as the law book and make sure that only Christians are the rulers. Some Christians have the idea that all we have to do is teach people the Ten Commandments, the Lord's Prayer, and Bible stories, and we will turn America back into a Christian nation. However, we never were a Christian nation, nor shall we ever be one. Also, some other Christians think the so-called nation of Israel will someday soon be the headquarters on earth of the restored kingdom of God.

The Lord Jesus, however, tells us that His kingdom comes a different way. Remember what Jesus said when he was on trial before Pontius Pilate? "My kingdom is not of this world." Pilate understood that this kingdom was not a threat to him or Rome — a kingdom of the next world is a kingdom of the dead, and a king of dead people can't hurt Rome! So Pilate was ready to let Jesus go. And it is still true to this day that the kingdom of heaven is not of this world. It hasn't been and won't ever be. Jesus said so.

The Apostle Paul tells us what the kingdom of heaven really is, in the letter he wrote to the Colossians: "For [the Father] has rescued us from the dominion of darkness and brought us into the kingdom of the Son he loves, in whom we have redemption, the forgiveness of sins." These words imply that the kingdom of heaven already exists — but not as a country or political area. A world map shows a couple hundred countries. But God knows of only two world governments: the dominion of darkness — which is ruled by Satan — and the kingdom of Jesus. The Bible teaches us that all people start out in the dominion of darkness, no matter what form of government may rule the land they live in.

Now, we cannot move from the devil's dominion to the kingdom of heaven just because we want to. Just as certain diseases and mental illnesses and a criminal past disqualify people from immigrating to America, sin disqualifies people from the kingdom of heaven. Just as citizens of America don't want diseased, crazy, or criminal people allowed into our country because those people are a threat to us, would you want to live forever in heaven with people who are like the way they are now? Of course not! That would be hell, wouldn't it!

Now, as soon as we stop being sinners, we can enter into heaven — but that's like telling a person with AIDS or who has a criminal record, "You can immigrate into America once you are healed of AIDS or you are no longer a convicted criminal." Of course, that's impossible. And it is even more impossible for sinners to enter into heaven.

However, King Jesus led a daring raid on that dominion to liberate the people who live in darkness. In 1991, America led forces that liberated Kuwait, using the latest in modern machines and methods. We liberate with a show of force — but how do the countries look after we "liberate" them? A mess, right? Jesus, however, liberated us by removing our sins through redemption. We are better off when He gets done liberating us. "God brought us into the kingdom of the Son He loves, in whom we have redemption, the forgiveness of sins." That forgiveness qualifies us for citizenship in His kingdom. All we have to do is trust the invitation Jesus gives us to live with Him — and He even gives us the faith to do that!

The kingdom of heaven, then, does not come by military force, nor by legal action. It comes wherever the Holy Spirit gives people the faith to believe the forgiveness of sins Jesus offers. The kingdom of heaven is still not of this world — it will never show up as some kind of government. It is, as Jesus teaches us, among those who trust Him — the Christian Church. That's how God answers the prayer, "Thy kingdom come": by sending the church with the good news about Jesus. Americans are scattered across the globe in different lands — but they remain Americans. In a greater way, the kingdom of heaven is spread across the world, wherever someone is telling someone else about redemption and forgiveness. In fact, the Bible says that we are ambassadors for Christ. That means we have the authority to let people into the kingdom of heaven.

Now, even though you will never see the kingdom of heaven on earth because it is in the hearts of Christians, the kingdom of heaven will have some visible effect. Paul prayed, "We [ask] God to fill you with the knowledge of his will through all spiritual wisdom and understanding ... that you may live a life worthy of the Lord and may please him in every way ... who has qualified you to share in the inheritance of the saints in the kingdom of light." As we get to know our King Jesus better, His Spirit will change our lives. This also shows the presence of God's kingdom. But the main proof of the existence of the kingdom of God is wherever the word about Jesus is preached and His sacraments are used. So the kingdom of God is coming to you right now as you read this or gather in church or Bible study!

Prayer: Lord Jesus, fill us with the knowledge of Your will through all spiritual wisdom and understanding. Help us live a life worthy of Your name and please You in every way. Help us bear fruit in every good work, as we grow in the knowledge of God. Help us bear fruit in every good work, as we are strengthened with all power according to Your glorious might. Help us bear fruit in every good work so that we may have great endurance and patience, and joyfully give thanks to the Father, who has qualified us to share in the inheritance of the saints in the kingdom of light. Amen.

Object lesson: What is the main difference between a king and the President of the United States? A king is born to the job, while a president is elected to the job by the people.

Why does the Bible call Jesus our king when we live in America, which doesn't have any kings? Because we are also citizens of the kingdom of heaven, which is bigger than the United States.

What is the kingdom of heaven? It's another name for the Christian Church. Christians are the citizens of this kingdom.

How did we become citizens of the kingdom of heaven? The same way we became citizens of the United States: by birth. We were "born again" when we were baptized.

So we are citizens of two kingdoms — the kingdom of heaven and the United States of America. What's the difference between the duties we have as citizens of the United States and the duties we have as citizens of the kingdom of heaven? Americans have the duty to pay taxes, defend their homeland from enemies, and obey the laws of the land. Christians have the duty to tell other people about their king, Jesus, and to obey His commandments. We go to school to learn how to be good citizens of the United States. God's Holy Spirit helps us do our duty by teaching us about Jesus and giving us faith and courage to do our duty whenever we gather to learn about Jesus.

Psalm 115:1-18
1 Timothy 2:1-4
John 6:28-40

37. The Third Petition: Thy Will Be Done

> **THE LORD'S PRAYER — THE THIRD PETITION**
> Thy will be done on earth as it is in heaven. *What does this mean?* The good and gracious will of God is done indeed without our prayer; but we pray in this petition that it may be done among us also. *How is this done?* When God breaks and hinders every evil counsel and will which would not let us hallow God's name nor let His kingdom come, such as the will of the devil, the world, and our flesh; but strengthens and preserves us steadfast in His Word and faith unto our end. This is His gracious and good will.

Some people have strange ideas about God's will. A guy gets up in the morning and seeks what God's will is for the clothes he will wear that day —"Does God want me to wear the blue suit or the gray one?" When tragedy strikes, like when the crash of a small plane kills an entire family, an argument breaks out. Was it God's will that the plane crashed? Did the devil pull a fast one on God and keep God's will from being done? Or how about the argument that has split the church for the last 500 years: Some believe it is God's will that some people be saved and that it is God's will that the rest go to hell.

The Bible does tell us how God answers the prayer, "Thy will be done." The Apostle Paul wrote these words to a young pastor named Timothy: "God ... wills that all men be saved and to come to a knowledge of the truth." God's will is that all people be saved. Jesus said it this way: "I have come down from heaven not to do my will but to do the will of him who sent me. And this is the will of him who sent me, that I shall lose none of all that he has given me, but raise them up at the last day. For my Father's will is that everyone who looks to the Son and believes in him shall have eternal life, and I will raise him up at the last day."

That clearly answers the question, "Does God want people to go to hell?" The answer is no. "God wants everyone to be saved and come to a knowledge of the truth." "[Jesus] is the way, the truth and the life." "God wants everyone who looks to Jesus Christ to be saved." Clearly, God wants everyone to know and trust Jesus Christ. You are a Christian because God wanted you to know Jesus and be saved. You are not a Christian because you wanted to be Christian. We can't want to be Christian unless God gives us the ability to want that — "faith comes by hearing what is preached about Christ." God's will is done, then, first when Christians take the message of Jesus to the world around them.

Of course, the devil doesn't want that to happen, so he will throw up all kinds of walls and traps to keep us from doing God's will. He will stir up governments to persecute Christians. It's already started in this country in many places. Government policies are created to make it hard for Christians to have free speech. The devil will stir up our neighbors to ridicule and oppose us. Consider how television and other entertainment forms portray Christians — as kooks, nuts, or dangerous hypocrites. The devil will try to use our human nature to distract us from doing God's will by laying temptations before us that seem more pleasurable than God's work.

Many times those temptations are sinful, like being a thief, fornicator, or adulterer. It's hard to do God's will — it's hard to tell others about Jesus and forgiveness of sins — if one is living a clearly sinful life. However, temptations can also be things that are good, but that distract us from doing God's will, from telling others about Jesus. For example, spending time with our families is good and so is working hard at our jobs. But the devil will say, do fun things with the family — and going to church is no fun, especially for the kids. Work hard, seven days a week, so you are too tired or busy to go to church. The devil will do anything to distract us from doing God's will of telling others about Christ.

Since the devil is working hard to undercut God's will, God must also deal with him, as well as the world and our sinful human nature, if God will get His will done. Jesus offers us Himself as bread from heaven. He feeds our souls so that they will live forever. The more of this supernatural food we eat — which we do as we gather to hear about Jesus and use His sacraments — the easier it will be for us to resist the devil's temptations. We will be able to give honor to God's name by what we say and do, and we will be able to help Jesus save more lost sinners by going out and telling them about salvation. In short, it is as Dr. Luther summarized, "God breaks and hinders every evil counsel and will which would not let us hallow God's name nor let his kingdom come, such as the will of the devil, the world, and our flesh; but strengthens and preserves us steadfast in his Word and faith unto our end. This is his gracious and good will."

We apply these thoughts in the way Paul challenges Timothy: "I urge, then, first of all, that requests, prayers, intercession and thanksgiving be made for everyone — for kings and all those in authority, that we may live peaceful and quiet lives in all godliness and holiness." Pray that God would work with the rulers so we can do God's will unhindered. Pray that God would give us free course to preach His Word. God allows us to do whatever we want to do as long as what we do allows us to tell others about Jesus. Obviously, bank robbers and other criminals would have a hard time doing God's will. Any sin is outside the will of God. Sin blocks people from hearing us.

However, work as a farmer, housewife, student, or any other honest labor can be done according to God's will. The farmer who raises his crops so he can use some of the profits to pay for the work of the kingdom is farming according to God's will. On the other hand, a farmer or the like who never has time or money for kingdom work isn't doing God's will. The same is true for a housewife, a student, or any other thing we do in life. If we seek opportunity to tell others about Christ, we are doing it according to God's will. If we do these things just to enjoy life, we are doing them outside God's will. We need to keep our priorities straight. We don't have to think about Jesus every hour of the day. It's how and why we do what we do that shows us doing God's will.

Prayer: Lord Jesus, help us keep our priorities straight. Forgive us when we let Your will become a low priority in our lives. Help us make choices each day that allow us freedom to tell the good news You have left us here to tell. Give us Your Spirit so we may resist the temptations of the devil, who wants us to do anything but live holy lives and give testimony about You. Bless Your Word as it goes out through preaching and the sacraments. Bless pastors and teachers with faith that they may teach us Your will. And bless the time we spend at our daily tasks so that we may have opportunity to tell others of Your grace and mercy. Amen.

Proverbs 30:7-9
1 Timothy 6:17-19
John 6:44-51

38. The Fourth Petition: Give Us This Day Our Daily Bread

> **THE LORD'S PRAYER — THE FOURTH PETITION**
> Give us this day our daily bread. *What does this mean?* God gives daily bread indeed without our prayer, also to all the wicked; but we pray in this petition that He would lead us to know it, and to receive our daily bread with thanksgiving. *What is meant by daily bread?* Everything that belongs to the support and wants of the body, such as food, drink, clothing, shoes, house, home, field, cattle, money, goods, a pious spouse, pious children, pious servants, pious and faithful rulers, good government, good weather, peace, health, discipline, honor, good friends, faithful neighbors, and the like.

I believe that most people think they don't get enough money for what work they do. I hear farmers complain about the price of grain and how it is still selling for about the same price it was when their dads were farming. Union workers regularly go on strike to get higher wages and more benefits. Sit around the coffee shop long enough and you will hear complaints that local businessmen and merchants pay unfairly low wages, making a fat profit on the sweat of oppressed workers. Added to that, coffee shop talk complains that not enough paycheck is left at the end of the month, taxes are too high, wages are too low, and expenses are on the rise. Even preachers complain — a common joke they tell is how churches pray to God to give them poor and humble preachers. "You keep them humble, Lord, and we'll keep them poor." If you are like me, you have probably looked to heaven and said to God, "God, I can't make it on what I have — I need more."

However, when we pray "give us this day our daily bread," we are challenged to trust God like a wise man named Agur did. In his proverb is a strange prayer: "Give me neither poverty nor riches, but give me only my daily bread. Otherwise, I may have too much and disown you and say, 'Who is the LORD?' Or I may become poor and steal, and so dishonor the name of my God." In short, he prays, "Give me what I need to keep me honest and faithful — give me daily bread." Jesus taught us nothing new, then, in the Lord's Prayer! People had been praying that way for at least a thousand years.

Jesus Christ answers this prayer for us in two ways. First, He offers us bread that will give us eternal life. "I am the bread of life. Your forefathers ate the manna in the desert, yet they died. But here is the bread that comes down from heaven, which a man may eat and not die. I am the living bread that came down from heaven. If anyone eats of this bread, he will live forever." Jesus contrasted how God had provided miraculous food for Israel in the desert, but that food did not keep them alive forever. On the other hand, Jesus taught that He offered bread that would give eternal life. He taught that He was that bread.

So if a Christian starves to death, did he really? There is always the "last meal" we shall eat. When we eat it, we will then die — maybe right away, maybe the next day or a few weeks later, but sooner or later, we will die. No food will keep us alive forever. Or, what does a Christian lose if he goes bankrupt, or can't afford to live in a bigger house, or buy nicer clothes? As we use the Word and sacraments of Jesus, He feeds us food that helps us live forever! This is the first way Jesus answers the prayer, "Give us this day our daily bread." He gives us Himself.

Then, as a daily reminder of bread that lasts forever, Jesus sees to it that we have, as Dr. Luther summarizes, "everything that belongs to the support and wants of the body, such as food, drink, clothing, shoes, house, home, field, cattle, money, goods, a pious spouse, pious children, pious servants, pious and faithful rulers, good government, good weather, peace, health, discipline, honor, good friends, faithful neighbors, and the like." Everything that is good is part of how God answers the prayer, "Give us this day our daily bread." Who gave you that farm, that job, that house? The devil? Your own sweat and blood? There are people who work harder than you do who have less than you have. God sees to it that we have what we have. Only if we go outside God's will — by stealing — can we have more than what God gives us. Who puts our leaders in office? Voters? The devil? The two working together? Jesus told Pilate, "All authority comes from heaven." Jesus put our current president in office. He also put Hitler, Stalin and others like them in office — because they did offer law and order.

Maybe Jesus doesn't give the complete list of good things to everyone. But whatever He gives is enough to keep us going until He is ready to call us home to heaven with Him. Stack up what you have against what others have and you might see a different pile, but you have a pile. If it bothers you that God gives more to others than you, then read the newspaper and compare your pile to the ones God gave to people in Somalia, Ethiopia, and other places like that! Only those in the grave have nothing in this world — but even that's no problem if they are Christians!

How much daily bread is enough? What about starving Christians in Somalia or Ethiopia or India? What about Christians who live in Palestine, who have had their homes ruined by Israeli military attacks? While some of you might think that three-dollar wheat is bad news, what about those who have to pay twenty, thirty, forty dollars or more to get theirs? How much daily bread is enough? How many of you pay too much in taxes? Maybe you would like to be so poor that you didn't have to pay taxes. Do you think we pay the teachers and school administrators too much? Maybe you would like to live where there are no schools. Do you think that you are living below what you are worth? Maybe you would like to spend more of your time taking care of more property and paying more taxes on it. Would you like to live in a bigger house? Maybe you would like to have more rooms to vacuum, more walls to paint, more yard to mow. I think we often lie to ourselves about how well off we really are. Few of us are so poor we are tempted to steal to stay alive. Few of us are so poor we cannot be generous in offerings of time and money to do the work of God's kingdom. What we have too easily fools us into thinking that we should have more. We can too easily focus on what we don't have and forget what we do have.

If you are alive tomorrow, God answered your prayer for daily bread today. You are alive today as proof that God answered your prayer for daily bread yesterday! If you are dead tomorrow, you are with Jesus where He has stored up eternal treasures for you. Either way, you get your daily bread. Either way, you have something to be thankful for.

Prayer: O Lord Jesus, teach us to be thankful for what we have instead of unhappy about what we don't have. Help us believe that You will see to it we will survive this life and end up wealthy beyond our wildest hopes and dreams. Thank You for pastors and teachers who feed us the bread from heaven You serve us through Your suffering, death and resurrection from the dead. Fill us full with that bread so we will more easily enjoy and be thankful for the daily bread You give us in this life. Amen.

Psalm 32:1-6
Ephesians 4:30-32
Matthew 18:21-34

39. The Fifth Petition: Forgive Us Our Trespasses

> **THE LORD'S PRAYER — THE FIFTH PETITION**
> And forgive us our trespasses, as we forgive those who trespass against us. *What does this mean?* We pray in this petition that our Father in heaven would not look upon our sins, nor on their account deny our prayer; for we are worthy of none of the things for which we pray, neither have we deserved them; but that He would grant them all to us by grace; for we daily sin much and indeed deserve nothing but punishment. So will we also heartily forgive, and readily do good to, those who sin against us.

This past year, if someone had paid you ten dollars for every kind word you ever spoke about other people, and also collected five dollars for every unkind word, would you be rich or poor? Isn't it true that we often find it easier to cut somebody up than to build him up? I am surrounded by a bunch of angry, resentful, and nasty people. So are you. Some of you are in the crowd of critics that surrounds me. And, God forgive me, I am in the crowd that surrounds some of you. "But I have a right to be angry!" Human nature naturally resents bad treatment. Human nature also seeks to even the score when treated badly. Don't we have an old saying: Don't get mad — get even? The result of all this spills over into the church. Why else would the Apostle Paul write, "Get rid of all bitterness, rage and anger, brawling and slander, along with every form of malice"? Pastors tell horror stories of terrorist attacks during voters' meetings, of members who are fire-breathing dragons. Church members grumble among themselves about each other and have even been known to quit coming to church because they are mad at somebody.

What should be done about those nasty people who get on your nerves and make life miserable for you? There once was a man who had a hard time getting along with people. The members of the church he grew up in threw him out one day because they considered him to be an arrogant heretic — some even tried to kill him, they were so mad at him. He went from church to church but usually ended up in a fight with the pastor. Soon, this man was fighting with the church leadership, accusing them of being corrupt. Church leadership, on the other hand, considered this guy to be a dangerous nut, a troublemaker. Sparks flew whenever this man showed up. Church leadership decided that something had to be done. They secretly put out a contract on this guy offering a reward to the person who would deliver this troublemaker into their hands dead or alive. Eventually, church leaders successfully managed to lynch this troublemaker. But as nails were being pounded into the hands and feet of Jesus of Nazareth, He looked into heaven and prayed for those church leaders and those finishing the grisly execution: "Father, forgive them."

What church leaders did with Jesus is what we like to do with each other, isn't it? In small ways we like to crucify each other — or at least beat each other up like the Romans did Jesus before executing Him. But notice how Jesus treats those who treated Him badly. He could have called down legions of angels — one of which could wipe out a city of a couple hundred thousand people. He could have spoken a word, like those He spoke to demons or storms, and melted His enemies into a puddle. With a touch of the hand that healed lepers and raised the dead Jesus could have slapped His tormentors into orbit. Jesus looked at those nasty people who were always getting on His nerves and making life miserable for Him … and forgave them. Jesus was more than willing to let bygones be bygones. He was also willing to give these people a place in His eternal kingdom.

This is still true. We today are of the same sort of people who stood around the cross of Jesus. They all had things in common — sinfulness, rebellion, wickedness. A few were different, however.

They admitted their sinfulness and grieved over the horrible treatment their Lord endured. A few days later, that grief turned to everlasting joy when they saw Jesus alive again and realized that He still loved them and had a place for them in His kingdom. Jesus forgave Peter's denials, Thomas' doubts. Later, Jesus forgave the murder and violence Paul had worked on Christians. Today, He forgives my failures and yours — and still holds open a place for us to rule with him in His everlasting kingdom!

A friend of Clara Barton, founder of the American Red Cross, once reminded Clara of an especially cruel thing that someone did to her years before. But Miss Barton seemed not to recall it. "Don't you remember it?" her friend asked. "No," came the reply, "I distinctly remember forgetting it." You can't be free and happy if you harbor grudges, so put them away. Get rid of them. Collect postage stamps, or collect coins, if you wish, but don't collect grudges. The Apostle Paul challenges us, "Get rid of all bitterness, rage and anger, brawling and slander, along with every form of malice. Be kind and compassionate to one another, forgiving each other, just as in Christ God forgave you." Forgive, just as in Christ God forgave you — then we can have peace, we can do great things together, we can see a bit of heaven on earth.

Prayer: Lord Jesus, You have given us Your Spirit, the Spirit who sealed us for the day of redemption. Forgive us when we grieve the Holy Spirit of God by our anger and meanness towards each other. Help us to give up our grudges. Help us to soften our behavior towards each other. Help us to give up rudeness, bitterness. Teach us to speak well of each other, to be kind to each other, and to forgive each other with words and deeds of compassion. Help us show off to the world Your master plan of salvation by making us showcase examples of mercy and forgiveness. Amen.

Psalm 25:1-12
James 1:12-18
Matthew 4:1-11

40. The Sixth Petition: Lead Us Not Into Temptation

> **THE LORD'S PRAYER — THE SIXTH PETITION**
> And lead us not into temptation. *What does this mean?* God indeed tempts no one; but we pray in this petition that God would guard and keep us, so that the devil, the world, and our flesh may not deceive us nor seduce us into misbelief, despair, and other great shame and vice; and though we be assailed by them, that still we may finally overcome and obtain the victory.

A trial or temptation shows what kind of person one really is. In the Bible, those two words generally translate the same word in the original language. A trial or temptation reveals either the strengths or the weakness of whatever is being tested. The Apostle James tells us how temptation works: "God cannot be tempted by evil, nor does he tempt anyone; but each one is tempted when, by his own evil desire, he is dragged away and enticed. Then, after desire has conceived, it gives birth to sin; and sin, when it is full-grown, gives birth to death." Sinful desires give way to sinful deeds, which always end up killing the sinner. That's why we fail the tests that come our way. There is only one reason why I sin. I want to. Sure, the devil likes to team up with people around me to stir up my sinful desires, but he can't make me sin, and neither can anybody else. Sinful desires give way to sinful deeds, which always end up killing the sinner. Everybody fails the test! Death proves that.

The devil tries to find the cracks and weaknesses in my soul. These are in different places than they are in your souls. The weakness might be in self-control. It might be in faithfulness. It might

179

be in ambition. A skinny person looks at a fat person and wonders why the fat person can't have more self-control at the table. The fat person looks at the skinny person with a bad temper and wonders why the skinny person can't be as patient as he is. So the devil helps steer us into situations where he can stretch and strain our abilities, hoping to see us fail. He's like the child who bends a pencil to see how far he can go before it breaks. The test is over when the pencil is broken. Once he finds a weak spot, the devil will try to destroy you or me by repeating those temptations over and over. And he will have plenty of help from the world and our own sinful human natures.

The devil tried this on Jesus. First the devil tried to see if Jesus was selfish by tempting Jesus to turn stones to bread. Jesus passed the test by quoting Scriptures to show that he trusted God to take care of Him. Then the devil tried to see if Jesus really trusted God by inviting Jesus to jump off the nineteen-story-tall Temple. Jesus passed the test by quoting the Bible again, saying that it was not His job to test God. Next, the devil tried to see if Jesus was afraid of death by offering to make Jesus king without having to die on the cross. Jesus passed that test by sending the devil packing, saying that He would only worship God even if it meant suffering pain and death. The devil took one last shot at this as Jesus hung on the cross by stirring people in the crowd to dare Jesus to come down from the cross. "We'll believe in you if you come down!" Wasn't that a real test for Jesus? Didn't Jesus want people to trust Him? Jesus passed that test also.

The writer of the letter to the Hebrews says that Jesus was tested as we are in all things, except that He did not sin. That means Jesus endured the same kind of temptations we endure. He was tempted to lust, to steal, to lie, to cheat, to hate. But Jesus passed the tests. Because He did, we can be confident that He will answer our prayer, "Lead us not into temptation." First, we know that Jesus will never try to get us to sin. He doesn't have to test us to find our weaknesses. He already knows our weaknesses.

So Jesus will never lead us into temptation. But He will lead us through temptation. Jesus stands ready to help us past the tests the devil, the world, and our own sinful human natures like to throw our way. James tells us how: "He chose to give us birth through the word of truth, that we might be a kind of firstfruits of all he created." By nature, we like to sin. We like to fail the test. The only way we can pass the tests is to get a new nature, to start over, a birth through the word of truth. Remember, Jesus resisted the temptations of the devil by drawing on the strength found in God's Word. When enemies crushed Him, when cares of the world piled high on Him, He always retreated into God's Word.

James writes, "Blessed is the man who perseveres under trial, because when he has stood the test, he will receive the crown of life that God has promised to those who love him." If we will return daily to the promises God made to us in His Word and sacraments, we will find the strength to endure temptation. We will be able to pass the test, to overcome the devil, world, and flesh. We will also find blessing and eternal life.

Prayer: Lord Jesus, forgive us for blaming our sins on people around us. It's not their bad behavior that makes us sin. It's not the troubles we put up with that make us sin. We sin because we allow our sinful human nature to have its way in those situations. You have given us a new birth through Your Word and sacraments of baptism and Holy Communion. Help us draw strength from those blessings so that we may resist the temptations of the devil, the world, and our flesh. Guard and keep us, so that we may endure and overcome those temptations and finally obtain the victory You already have won! Amen.

Object lesson: Point to a bag marked "Temptation" and tell the children that there is a test inside. Take a candy bar from the bag and place it on a pew across the room from them. Pick two or three of the rowdiest children for a race. Say, "On your mark, get ready," but then pause long enough to get one or more of the children to do a false start. Tell them they have failed the test. (Give all a candy bar.) The real temptation was that I had the sack of candy bars in my office for part of the week!

The Bible tells us that we sin when we give in to temptation. But what is temptation? Temptation is a test of how we will act or talk or think. The devil likes to tempt us to do wrong. That means he likes to give us tests that he thinks we will fail — just as I knew that a candy bar prize would tempt children to try and start running for the candy bar before each other.

The devil likes to see us fail many different kinds of tests. He likes to see us get really angry at each other — that means we have failed to forgive. He likes to see us steal and cheat and tell lies — that means we have failed to trust God to take care of us. The devil likes to see children disobey their parents — that means that the children don't respect and honor their parents as they should. He likes to see us treat each other badly. He likes to see us fail to forgive.

Jesus is willing to forgive us when we fail the devil's tests. Jesus is also willing to help us pass the tests the next time they come. He does this by putting His Holy Spirit inside us as we go to Sunday school and church to hear the good news about Jesus.

Psalm 71:1-12
Romans 7:21-25
Luke 6:6-10

41. The Seventh Petition: Deliver Us From Evil

> **THE LORD'S PRAYER — THE SEVENTH PETITION**
> But deliver us from evil. *What does this mean?* We pray in this petition, as the sum of all, that our Father in heaven would deliver us from every evil of body and soul, property and honor, and finally, when our last hour has come, grant us a blessed end, and graciously take us from this vale of tears to Himself in heaven.

Imagine watching your house collapse into floodwater and wash away; imagine your source of income buried in fifteen feet of water for six months. You would then have a small idea of the evil that people along the Mississippi River valley went through the summer of 1993. Now think of a loved one lying in bed, dying of cancer. Think of a child, broken and bleeding because he was beat up by one of his parents. Think of the many victims of murder, rape, and violence whose stories we hear on the news. Headlines often point out some attack or disaster going on. Dictators still rule with an iron fist, and thumb their noses at the rest of the world. Police cannot stop the tidal wave of gang and racial violence. Evil is out of control. Meanwhile there are people standing by, waiting for God to do something about it and wondering why He doesn't.

"Deliver us from evil," we pray to God. How does He answer this prayer? We look around and it seems He is either not able or not interested in saving us from evil. There is so much of it in this world! We can join in the desperate prayer of helplessness found in Psalm 71: "My enemies speak against me, those who wait to kill me conspire together. They say, 'God has forsaken him; pursue him and seize him, for no one will rescue him.' "

There once was a man who had a shriveled hand. Everyone agreed that evil had struck this man. After all, don't most people think evil is anything we don't like? Yet the man went to church anyway, as so many people do, willing to take from the Lord whatever the Lord is willing to give. Then one day, a visiting preacher named Jesus of Nazareth stopped by that church. This preacher spotted the man with the crippled hand and felt sorry for him.

However, Jesus also noticed a few in the crowd casting a suspicious eye His way. Those people considered Jesus to be evil. They considered Jesus to be a dangerous cult leader like David Koresh or Jim Jones — an evil, dangerous deceiver. After all, they had already caught Jesus and His students harvesting a snack of grain on the Sabbath! A crime against God! And now it looked like Jesus might be willing to do some doctoring on the Sabbath! So Jesus, knowing what they were thinking, said to them, "Which is lawful to do on the Sabbath: to do good or evil, to save life or destroy it?" The answer is obvious, but goes against what the leaders wanted to say. Of course it is against the law to do evil on the Sabbath (or any day), but is it against the law to do good? Then, to answer His own question, Jesus healed the shriveled hand. "Reach out your hand," says Jesus. With a word, Jesus heals, and what could be evil about giving this man a downpayment of eternal life?

But that made folks mad at Jesus. He's damned if He does and damned if He doesn't. First, Jesus is damned if He does save people from evil because a whole crowd will complain that He didn't do it the way they wanted Him to do it. Then Jesus is damned if He doesn't. There will always be those who will complain that He saved others but neglected to save them. No wonder Jesus was crucified! That's what people did with the damned in those days. Crucifixion showed how cursed the damned was.

Yet Jesus did not stay dead, did He? Folks did the worst they could and Jesus walked away from it—and better off than before! They robbed Him, beat Him, spit on Him, ripped His flesh with whips and nails. They mocked Him, pierced Him, and strangled Him. But Jesus popped the lid off His grave and took His place at the right hand of the Father, as king of the universe! There this

Jesus waits to hear our prayer, and when we pray, "Deliver us from evil," the same grave-cracking power is aimed at whatever evil comes our way.

Obviously, then, when we are healthy, or when our property is safe, or when we are respected by people around us, we can thank Jesus for answering our prayer. However, what does it mean if Jesus, who commanded storms to shut up, doesn't stop floods from washing away homes and businesses? What does it mean when Jesus, who healed cripples and raised the dead, allows disease or injury to rob us of life? What does it mean when Jesus, who declares us to be saints, ignores those around us who tear us down? What does it mean when it looks like he is not delivering us from evil? It can only mean that He has a bigger plan in mind, one that will carry us safe and sound from this life to the next, like what happened to Him. God may wait until it looks like it is too late, when it is beyond our ability to do anything about the evil that has washed over us. Then He rolls up His sleeves and says, "Now watch," and He comes into the hopeless situation and makes us better off than before — as He did for Jesus when He raised Jesus from the dead and seated Him at His right side. Thus, when we pray "Deliver us from evil," the best answer obviously comes when we die in peace, knowing where we are going, and that we rise again and live with Him. But we also know that any deliverance we experience in this life is a downpayment on the greater deliverance which is yet to come. So, either way, we can't lose!

Prayer: Thank You, Almighty God, for surrounding us with Your power and might, so that the devil may not lay claim on us. Thank You for using Your power and might to keep us safe from many evils we never see. And thank You for showing us that You can turn the worst evil into the highest good. Help us believe these things because the world around us is so evil and we are threatened daily by it. Use us as messengers of hope to those who find themselves drowning in a sea of evil. And bring us all safe to that great reunion in heaven where we shall gather with all the saints to live forever free from evil. Amen.

Psalm 103:15-22
Romans 8:19-30
Luke 23:32-43

42. The Conclusion: Thine Is The Kingdom

> THE LORD'S PRAYER — THE CONCLUSION
> For Thine is the kingdom and the power and the glory forever and ever. Amen. *What is meant by the word "Amen"?* That I should be certain that these petitions are acceptable to our Father in heaven and are heard by Him; for He Himself has commanded us so to pray, and has promised to hear us. Amen, Amen, that is, Yea, yea, it shall be so.

Amen. That's one of those words in the Bible that has managed to find its way into all the languages of the world. In English, we would say, "You can depend on that." It's sort of like a chair; you don't ask yourself, "I wonder if this chair will support me?" — you assume it will, because it is a chair. How much more is this true of God? The Hebrew people would merely say, "Amen," to that dependability. Remember a number of times Jesus, in the old King James Bible, would say something like, "Amen, Amen, I say unto you"? That was His way of saying, "What I am about to say is most certainly true; it is something you can depend on."

Amen. Why do we put that at the end of our prayers? Because our prayers are dependable? No. That's our confession of faith in our God. And today I would like to focus specifically on how the word "Amen" is used in the Bible in a very special and unique way. Did you know that "Amen" is a nickname for Jesus? You can find this in the book of Revelation, where he says, "Tell the Laodiceans this is what the Amen says." So when we say our prayers and we end them with the word "Amen," we as Christians have in mind that our prayer can be prayed only because of Jesus, because he is the one that's dependable, not us. Often we also show this by saying just before "Amen" something like, "through Jesus Christ."

Now in the Lord's Prayer, we end by saying, "For Thine is the kingdom and the power and the glory forever and ever. Amen." But did you notice in the catechism when it comes to explaining that, it doesn't say anything about the kingdom and the power and the glory, does it? It just focuses on the word "Amen." That's because "Amen" summarizes "for Thine is the kingdom and the power and the glory." Remember, "Amen" talks about Jesus. It's His name. And if you look at those words there, "For Thine is the kingdom, the power and glory," they also point to Jesus. I'd like to focus especially on the connection between the words "For Thine is the kingdom" and "Amen."

"For Thine is the kingdom." Remember when Jesus was going around the countryside? What was he preaching about? The Gospel writers report that it was, "Repent, for the kingdom of God is at hand." Of course, He wasn't merely walking around saying, "Repent, for the kingdom of God is at hand" — that's just the summary of the message, that's the theme of His sermons that He went around preaching. His preaching was about His coming kingdom.

Now remember when Jesus was finally arrested by the chief priests, brought to trial before the supreme court of the Jews, what was the charge that was brought against Him? He was convicted of blasphemy. He was convicted of saying, "I am the Son of God." But also remember that the supreme court wanted Jesus executed, but they wanted the Romans to do the dirty work. And yet the supreme court recognized that if they took Jesus before Pontius Pilate and said, "This man deserves to die, because he says he is the Son of God," Pilate's going to laugh them right out of court. Romans worshiped many men who claimed to be gods. So, what charge did they take to Pontius Pilate against Jesus? They took one statement that Jesus made at his trial, "I am the Christ."

When Jesus said, "I am the Christ," His enemies knew that the Romans would be interested in that statement, because the word "Christ" is a loaded term. For centuries God's people had been looking forward to a Christ — God's "Anointed," a King — who would be their Savior. Along the way, they also began to believe that this king would come to defeat Rome, and would establish the Holy Land as the headquarters of God's government on earth.

This is what would catch Pilate's attention. Pilate would say, "A king? Nobody can be king unless he first swears allegiance to Rome. I don't want any kings running around who've got some idea that they're going to set up a kingdom that's going to overthrow the Romans." He already had two Jewish kings to contend with as it was. He had one Herod up in the north and another down in the south. Each claimed to be king of the Jews. The last thing he needed was some fellow running around claiming to be another king of the Jews.

So Pilate asks Jesus point-blank, "Are you the king of the Jews?" And what did Jesus say? "Yes. You said it. But my kingdom is not of this world." With those words, Pontius Pilate was able to breathe a big sigh of relief. "Not a king of this world? His kingdom must be in another world!" There's only one other world that Pilate knew about, the world where the dead go. So for Jesus to say that His kingdom was not of this world meant that Jesus' kingdom was of the next world, and what threat could that possibly be to Pilate or to Rome? To be king of the dead — so what? So Pilate was willing to let Jesus go.

Of course the Jews pressed Pilate, until finally he said, "All right, all right. I'll execute him. And I'll execute him as king of the Jews, just for you. But I'm also going to make you sorry that you messed with me. I'll show you what I think of your king — and what I think of you!" So Pilate let his soldiers dress Jesus up like a king, pay mock homage to Him, and then beat Him black and blue. Pilate made sure that, when Jesus was crucified, a sign over his head said, "This is the King of the Jews." Then, just to mock the Jews further, Pilate had two criminals crucified with Jesus — one on one side, and one on the other, the mocking image of a king and his court, the king with his criminal advisers on either side of him. By this, Pilate said what he thought of the kingdom of the Jews — it's a kingdom of robbers and thieves, of crooks and the worst of humankind.

So, there's Jesus hanging on the cross. On the left-hand side is a criminal who is mocking Jesus, "Save us, O king!" And on the right-hand side is a criminal who says, "Hey, we're getting what we deserve. This man is innocent." He turns to Jesus and says, "Jesus, remember me when you come into your kingdom." And how did Jesus answer that? "Today you will be with me in paradise." There, hanging on a cross, Jesus demonstrated what it meant when he went around preaching, "The kingdom of heaven is at hand." The kingdom of heaven is made up of people like that criminal who confess their unworthiness, who then receive Jesus' promise of eternal life. That's the kingdom.

Where's the "Amen"? As He died, He said, "It is finished." He said this after He prayed that the Father would forgive those who had executed Him and after He promised to take the penitent criminal to heaven with Him. "It is finished!" That's the "Amen" at the end of the prayer. "It is finished," Jesus told this malefactor. "Today you will be in paradise."

But that promise is only as good as the word of Jesus, isn't it? Yet, hasn't Jesus showed that His Word is dependable, that He is "Amen"? Only by death on a cross could He take away the sins of the world. He showed that He could be depended on when He went to that cross — and that's why we decorate our churches with crosses, to remind us of Jesus and His dependability.

And then God says "Amen" to what Jesus did for us, and what He promised to do for us, by raising Him again from the dead. Is there any question, then, that the kingdom of heaven belongs to God, through and in and from Christ? That's what the Bible means when it talks about the kingdom of God. It only means Jesus. It doesn't mean any political power here on earth, whether in Washington or in Jerusalem, as some people mistakenly think today; it has to do with Jesus and the message of forgiveness of sins. So the kingdom does not belong to our national leaders; it does not belong to the United Nations; it does not belong to any man who claims to be in charge of things. The kingdom belongs to the Father in heaven, in and through and from Jesus Christ the Amen. And that kingdom is found wherever the forgiveness of sins is declared and believed.

So here in this place is the kingdom of God. You people gathered here today are the kingdom of God. And the promise that Jesus made to this malefactor is the same promise He makes to you. "Today you will be with me in paradise." You can go straight from this room into the presence of God. And we do, don't we, in our prayers? We don't need priests. We don't need anything, because we have Jesus, God's Amen, who has opened the way for us. He is the King. And His forgiveness, His kingdom, is as dependable as what He has done for us. And so all we have to do is look back — what did He do? He suffered, He died, He rose again, He sits at the right hand of God. And that's what "Amen" is all about. Jesus rules heaven and earth for our sake. "All things work together for good for those who love the Lord." Why? Because Jesus is Amen; Jesus is the king. That's saying the same thing in two different ways.

Prayer: Lord Jesus, help us to believe that You are the king, and that Yours is the kingdom, especially when we look around us and we see how evil is out of control. Give us faith to depend on Your royal decree of forgiveness, and on how that royal decree transforms and changes fallen humankind into citizens fit for heaven. Make us fit for heaven as we hear that decree declared to us, and give us faith to come and live under that decree. All this we pray for Your precious name's sake. Amen.

Psalm 68:28-35
Romans 1:16-17
Luke 4:1-13

43. The Conclusion: Thine Is The Power

> THE LORD'S PRAYER — THE CONCLUSION
> For Thine is the kingdom and the power and the glory forever and ever. Amen. *What is meant by the word "Amen"?* That I should be certain that these petitions are acceptable to our Father in heaven, and are heard by Him; for He Himself has commanded us so to pray, and has promised to hear us. Amen, Amen, that is, Yea, yea, it shall be so.

God's people all through the ages have ended their prayers with "Amen." We learned in childhood that "Amen, Amen" means, "Yea, yea, it shall be so." From the book of Isaiah: "Whoever invokes a blessing in the land will do so by the God of Amen; he who takes an oath in the land will swear by the God of Amen." Amen is a name for God in the Old Testament. From the book of John's Revelation: "To the angel of the church in Laodicea write: These are the words of the Amen, the faithful and true witness, the ruler of God's creation." Amen is also a name for Jesus Christ, because it is Jesus who speaks in this passage. We end our prayers with "Amen" because we are certain that God wants us to pray — He's the God of Amen — and promises to hear us as we are certain about Jesus Christ — who is also our Amen.

On October 31, 1517, a young Roman Catholic monk named Martin Luther nailed 95 statements on the bulletin board of his church. These 95 statements called into question practices and beliefs popular in the church of his day. In short, Luther challenged the claim that popes alone had the power to open heaven or to delegate that authority. He claimed Jesus alone had such power.

Martin Luther was a student of the Bible. His studies led him to notice that the Bible said one thing about how a person gets into heaven — how a person gets right with God — while the church headquarters in faraway Rome taught something else. The pope claimed that he had authority from heaven to open or close heaven. He also taught that he could sell that authority. Seems he needed lots of money to hire Michelangelo to oversee the construction of the church in Rome. Now, this was a good fundraising technique, because a lot of people want to have their sins forgiven, and here comes this merchant to town who is selling forgiveness of sins. He bought that authority from the pope in Rome. He then would ask what kind of sins you needed forgiven — or what kind of sins your relatives needed forgiven (including those who were already dead).

But Luther came across what Paul wrote in his letter to the Romans, "I am not ashamed of the gospel, because it is the power of God for the salvation of everyone who believes." From this and other Scriptures, Luther concluded that any person who believes this thing called the gospel will find that the gospel has all the power it takes to save him — that he doesn't need popes or priests to clear the way for him.

What is the gospel Saint Paul wrote of, in which Luther also put his faith? The Gospel of Mark begins with these words: "The beginning of the gospel about Jesus Christ, the Son of God." The rest of the book tells us about the work of Jesus Christ. But the apostle himself defines what he means by "gospel" earlier in the letter. "Paul, a servant of Christ Jesus, called to be an apostle and set apart for the gospel of God — the gospel he promised beforehand through his prophets in the Holy Scriptures regarding his Son, who as to his human nature was a descendant of David, and who through the Spirit of holiness was declared with power to be the Son of God by his resurrection from the dead: Jesus Christ our Lord." The gospel clearly is that story about Jesus Christ, which we find unfolded for us in the Old Testament, which describes the death and resurrection of Jesus Christ. The power of salvation is found in a message!

In our day and age, power is measured by how much money one has, how big an army a country has, how much strength a person can show. When a country goes to war, its leaders mass manpower and machines to overwhelm the enemy. When a bank robber holds hostages, police sharpshooters surround the place in a show of force. It would seem logical, then, that if God wanted to save humankind from the devil, God would have to overpower the devil with some show of force.

That's where Jesus Christ fits. Remember what happened when Jesus and the devil first met face to face? Jesus was in the desert for forty days being tempted by the devil. What did Jesus do? How did He turn back the temptations of the devil? He quoted Bible passages! Later, Jesus allowed the forces of evil to do the worst they could to Him, and then undid all the evil, making things better than they were in the first place. Jesus allowed evil people to harass Him, to torture Him, and finally to murder Him. But then Jesus popped the lid off His grave, unharmed, and now rules the universe at the right hand of the Father.

In an unexpected display of power, at least one that is still unexpected in this world, that a person would show his strength by allowing himself to be completely humiliated and defeated—Jesus showed that God's strength is complete in what some people call weakness. In particular, Jesus showed that God's Word has all the power we need to break the devil's hold over us. All it takes to defeat the devil is God's saying something. So it is the power of God's Word that we focus on. In fact, because Jesus is God's Word, dressed in flesh and blood, Jesus is all we need to rescue us from evil.

All that power for salvation is packed into the stories we tell about Jesus. As we unfold the Scriptures and look to see what the Scriptures have to say about Jesus, there is the power of God for salvation at work. That's what Paul meant when he tells us, "The gospel is the power of God for the salvation of everyone who believes." We don't need slick marketing tricks or to turn the church into a variety show to add souls to the kingdom of heaven. It is the gospel alone that makes the church grow. "For in the gospel a righteousness from God is revealed." All we need is the good news that Jesus is Lord and Savior, that He suffered, died, rose again and sits at the right hand of the Father. When I am tempted to trade that gospel for worldly techniques, I remember the words of Paul that it is the gospel that is the power of salvation for those who believe. Our salvation is as sure as Jesus Christ. Is Jesus someone we can trust? Why not! Isn't he Amen? Isn't His power over sin, death, and the power of the devil the Amen we base our prayers on? We can be confident that He answers our prayers for salvation through His gospel. Where do we find this gospel? In His Word and sacraments, into which He puts His promise of salvation.

Prayer: Lord Jesus, in power You brought forth the heavens and the earth. In power You broke the devil's stranglehold on humankind by Your death on the cross. In power, You convert evil into blessing for those whom You have called. Forgive us when we become impressed with the power we see people show, whether it is scientific power or social power or whatever. Help us say Amen to Your power. Help us depend on You for truth and life. Help us believe that You are a mighty fortress and shield against all that is evil. Amen.

Isaiah 40:1-5
Romans 6:1-4
John 17:1-10

44. The Conclusion: Thine Is The Glory

> THE LORD'S PRAYER — THE CONCLUSION
> For Thine is the kingdom and the power and the glory forever and ever. Amen. *What is meant by the word "Amen"?* That I should be certain that these petitions are acceptable to our Father in heaven, and are heard by Him; for He Himself has commanded us so to pray, and has promised to hear us. Amen, Amen, that is, Yea, yea, it shall be so.

What do we mean when we say to our Father in heaven, "For Thine is the glory. Amen"? Luke tells a story about Jesus that shows us what glory is. Luke reports a time Jesus was invited to a dinner, and He noticed that as guests arrived, some headed straight for places of honor. So He said to some fellow dinner guests, "When someone invites you to a wedding feast, do not take the place of honor, for a person more distinguished than you may have been invited. If so, the host who invited both of you will come and say to you, 'Give this man your seat.' Then, humiliated, you will have to take the least important place. But when you are invited, take the lowest place, so that when your host comes, he will say to you, 'Friend, move up to a better place.' Then you will have glory in the presence of all your fellow guests. For everyone who exalts himself will be humbled, and he who humbles himself will be exalted." Notice: the person sitting in the place of honor has glory in the eyes of the other guests. Notice also that glory is joined to being exalted, lifted up in the eyes of people. In fact, this is what lay behind what Jesus later told his host: "When you make glory, invite the poor, the crippled, the lame, the blind, and you will be blessed." "Making glory" meant throwing a party for a guest of honor. Don't throw a party to honor someone who can turn around and do the same for you. Instead, invite those who do not have honor in the eyes of the people, who can't invite you to a party thrown in your honor, and God will honor you. Glory, then, is what a guest of honor at a dinner has. Think about dinners that have a guest of honor. The master of ceremonies goes on and on about all the great accomplishments of the guest of honor.

So, what are we saying when we pray, "For Thine is the glory. Amen"? If we remember that "Amen" is one of the names of Jesus, and that glory is what an honored guest has at a wedding feast or dinner, then we can imagine the kind of dinner where Jesus is the guest of honor. And here is some of the glory Jesus would have. John tells how Jesus turned water into wine. John then wrote, "This, the first of his miraculous signs, Jesus performed at Cana in Galilee. He thus revealed his glory, and his disciples put their faith in him." Later, when Jesus heard that His friend Lazarus was dying, He said, "This sickness will not end in death. No, it is for God's glory so that God's Son may be glorified through it." At the grave, He told one of the weeping sisters, "Did I not tell you that if you believed, you would see the glory of God?" Then He showed that glory by raising Lazarus from the dead. John also reports that the evening before Jesus died, He prayed to the heavenly Father: "Father, the time has come. Glorify your Son, that your Son may glorify you. I have brought you glory on earth by completing the work you gave me to do. And now, Father, glorify me in your presence with the glory I had with you before the world began." Jesus prays that as He had brought glory to the Father by all the miracles He did in the Father's name, that now the Father would restore Jesus to the glory He once had in heaven. God answered that prayer by raising Jesus from the dead. What greater boost to one's reputation can one have than that! This is the greatest glory of Jesus. Clearly, the glory which Jesus enjoys is wrapped up in all the miracles He performed, especially when He came back from the dead. And this is the glory that Jesus shares with the Father in heaven. After all, didn't Paul write that it was by the glory of the Father that Jesus was raised from the dead?

Did you know that we share in the glory of God, that we are honored guests with an invitation to a dinner thrown in our honor? Paul writes, "Don't you know that all of us who were baptized into Christ Jesus were baptized into his death? We were therefore buried with him through baptism into death in order that, just as Christ was raised from the dead by the glory of the Father, we too may live a new life." John the Baptist once said, "I baptize you with water for repentance. But after me will come one who is more powerful than I, whose sandals I am not fit to carry. He will baptize you with the Holy Spirit and with fire." Jesus said, "Therefore go and make disciples of all nations, baptizing them in the name of the Father and of the Son and of the Holy Spirit." Paul also wrote, "You are all sons of God through faith in Christ Jesus, for all of you who were baptized into Christ have clothed yourselves with Christ." Notice what these Scriptures all say about baptism, how baptism is the kind of power God used to raise Jesus from the dead, that baptism has the power to cleanse someone. Notice how baptism gives you a new identity as we are clothed in Christ. Notice, then, that baptism is one of the great glories, great accomplishments, of Jesus Christ, that through baptism, a humble bowl of water, Jesus reaches out into the world and gathers to himself people like you and me. A sinner is crucified and brought back to life at each baptism. Each baptism gets rid of sin; each baptism makes a person like Jesus by clothing us in His righteousness.

Jesus once said, "I confer on you a kingdom, just as my Father conferred one on me, so that you may eat and drink at my table in my kingdom and sit on thrones, judging the twelve tribes of Israel." Think of the picture painted here. Here's the great King, and every time He throws a state dinner, whom does He invite to that dinner? Why, of course, He is going to invite His top government officials, as well as any other guests of honor. You have that invitation! Jesus says, "You will eat with me and you will rule with me." We have become government officials in the kingdom of God because of our baptism. The world may not recognize that, but so what? They may not see the glory that the Father has given us through Christ, but because of baptism, we are invited to eat at the banquet table of the King, our Lord Jesus. Someday we shall all be guests of honor at a banquet served by Jesus. He will stand us up in front of the world and He will say to us in front of all who despised and hated us, "Well done, good and faithful servant! You have been faithful over little. I will put you over much. When I was hungry you fed me, when I was thirsty you gave me a drink, when I was naked you clothed me, when I was in prison or sick in bed, you visited me." Then He will give us honor for that. That will be our glory in the face of the whole world. Folks, all this comes as answer to our prayer, "For Thine is the glory. Amen."

What else does Paul say about the glory we share with Jesus in our baptism? "I consider that our present sufferings are not worth comparing with the glory that will be revealed in us." So those of you who have been through terrible times, the more terrible those times have been, they are nothing compared to the glory that will soon be revealed in you when you stand before Jesus. Paul also wrote, "We speak of God's secret wisdom, a wisdom that has been hidden and that God destined for our glory before time began." The church has the job of letting the world know the secrets of God. As we do that, letting people know the grand plan God has for this world, we are accomplishing something great — something so great that the world will one day have to congratulate us for it! And God set this up to happen long before time began. Paul also wrote, "So will it be with the resurrection of the dead. The body is sown in dishonor, it is raised in glory." We know what it means to sow the body in dishonor. We see that cold, dead, lifeless body; we see it locked up in a box and put in the ground, and we think that's the saddest thing that can happen to a person in this life. And it makes no difference — rich or poor, famous or not — we all end up the same. The richest and most famous end up as the poorest and most unknown person — sown in dishonor. But those who are in Christ are raised in glory! We look forward to the time when our bodies are no longer subjected to the ravages of age and sin and death. Finally, the apostle also wrote, "And we, who with unveiled faces all reflect the Lord's glory, are being transformed into his likeness with ever-increasing glory, which comes from the Lord, who is the Spirit." What two things does he say about us? First, that because we are Christians, we already reflect the glory of Jesus. We already reflect the great accomplishment that Jesus has done. The fact that we are Christians is a great accomplishment, a miracle that can only be done by Jesus Himself. We are not Christians because we chose to be Christians, but because Jesus chose us. Then Paul goes on to say that we are being transformed into the likeness of the Lord, through ever-increasing glory; that as the Holy Spirit works on us, He is making us to be more and more like Jesus. So we can expect that as we get to know Jesus better — as we go to church, go to Sunday school, study our Bibles — we can also expect that we will become more like Jesus! Repentance gets easier. The day will come when we will enjoy the recognition and congratulation because of the change which Jesus has worked in us.

Prayer: O glorious One, Father in heaven, hear us as we pray in the name of Your glorious Son. Your mercy has overflowed on us in a shower of glory we share with Jesus. Though our sins are many, You drown them in baptism by the glorious power that raised Jesus from the dead. Though our bodies waste away because of the curse of death, we eagerly look forward to new and glorious bodies which You have promised. In the meantime, forgive us when we resist Your Spirit's efforts to change us until we are like Jesus. Stamp Your glory on us so that others will be attracted to the gospel of glory we preach. Amen.

Isaiah 25:1-9
Revelation 3:14-22
Matthew 19:23-30

45. The Conclusion: Amen

> **THE LORD'S PRAYER — THE CONCLUSION**
> For Thine is the kingdom and the power and the glory forever and ever. Amen. *What is meant by the word "Amen"?* That I should be certain that these petitions are acceptable to our Father in heaven, and are heard by Him; for He Himself has commanded us so to pray, and has promised to hear us. Amen, Amen, that is, Yea, yea, it shall be so.

Many years ago, when he was still in the seminary, a friend of mine visited a woman who was dying of lung cancer. Some friends had told her that all she had to do was pray and believe, and God would heal her. The day came when he arrived in her hospital room only a couple days before she actually died. Then, she looked up at him and said, "I cannot pray anymore." She had gotten mixed up with the "name it and claim it" crowd. They have the false idea that if you have enough faith, you can ask God for anything, and he will do it. So here's this precious child of God on her deathbed. She had tried so hard to pray in faith that God would spare her. But the doctors had told her she had a day or so left. So, she was convinced that she did not have the faith it took to pray.

What does one say to a person whose faith has been crushed by such a lie? All my friend could think of was what Jesus once said about prayer. So he took her hand and said, "Jesus said, 'When you pray, say "Our Father who art in heaven."' Jesus said, 'When you pray,' not 'if you have enough faith to pray.' And He said, 'Pray like this, "Our Father ..."' Jesus gave you that prayer. You can always pray it, no matter what." And they did pray that prayer together. No matter what, we can always pray the prayer our Lord taught us. That's because the great Amen taught it to us. And because our Father is King, we know that our prayers are heard. For that, we especially can be thankful. "Amen, Amen, that is, Yea, yea, it shall be so" is the grateful response that springs from a heart that trusts God always to do what is good and right for us.

But do we really mean it when we say Amen? Do we really believe that Jesus will take care of us as the Father's personal representative? What about when things go wrong and don't turn out as we expected? How can we be thankful when so often things don't turn out the way we want them to? Sometimes we just get done saying thanks, only to turn around and complain about what we didn't get or what we got that we really didn't want.

Where can we find the ability to thank God no matter what happens to us? How can we say Amen and really mean it? Consider what the ancient prophet Isaiah had to say. Isaiah sings, "O Lord, you are my God; I will exalt you and praise your name, for in perfect faithfulness you have done marvelous things, things planned long ago." Nowhere do we see this more than in the death and resurrection of Jesus from the dead. Foretold by prophets and sung by poets, God relentlessly set in motion events in human history that all aimed to land Jesus of Nazareth on a cross at just the right time. Not only so, but because Jesus now lives forever, He can see His plans completed exactly as He wished. He will either send good things our way, or change the evil things into blessings according to the power by which He governs all things for the good of the church. He sees a kingdom prepared for each of us from before the foundation of the world. There He has stored up treasures that cannot be stolen or spoiled. Jesus is God's Amen to us that we have a glorious future ahead of us, no matter what may happen now.

Isaiah sings, "You have made the city a heap of rubble, the fortified town a ruin, the foreigners' stronghold a city no more; it will never be rebuilt. Therefore strong peoples will honor you; cities of ruthless nations will revere you." Jesus lasts longer than our enemies, and wins over them eventually. Even sickness and death cannot hold us for long. What have we to fear from lesser enemies, like pestilence, famine, and persecution? Hell's gates are broken down, the devil's throne shattered. Standing in the rubble is an empty cross, stained with the blood of Christ. But it is empty, because Jesus Christ died there to destroy death by destroying its power, sin, and rose again to life to show how we are raised to new life in baptism. We can be thankful that Jesus as the Amen God speaks to us to assure us we shall survive this evil world.

Isaiah sings, "You have been a refuge for the poor, a refuge for the needy in his distress, a shelter from the storm and a shade from the heat. For the breath of the ruthless is like a storm driving against a wall and like the heat of the desert. You silence the uproar of foreigners; as heat is reduced by the shadow of a cloud, so the song of the ruthless is stilled." We have to put up with crooks and thieves and all manner of evil people as long as we live. Yet we can be thankful to know that Jesus has the last laugh on our enemies, because Jesus is God's Amen to us that He will put an end to all that is evil.

Isaiah sings on, "On this mountain the Lord Almighty will prepare a feast of rich food for all peoples, a banquet of aged wine — the best of meats and the finest of wines." Food is a big part of our Thanksgiving celebrations. No greater feast has been prepared than what Jesus lays before us — bread of life we eat as we hear His Word, His own body and blood offered to us for forgiveness of sins, water that springs up to eternal life from within us. We can be thankful for eternal food — Word and sacraments. As we eat and drink, we say Amen to the promise that we shall join with angels and archangels and all the company of heaven around heavenly food.

Isaiah's song of thanksgiving continues, "On this mountain he will destroy the shroud that enfolds all peoples, the sheet that covers all nations; he will swallow up death forever. The Sovereign Lord will wipe away the tears from all faces; he will remove the disgrace of his people from all the earth. The Lord has spoken." For some of you this year will be the first Thanksgiving without a loved one. Holidays have a way of reminding us of who is missing in our lives. And that hole is hard to fill. But I am here today with all of you who have lost loved ones to give thanks to Jesus who has undone the foreverness of death and given us a forever hope to look forward to. The Lord has spoken, and Jesus is that Word made flesh. He is God's eternal Amen to us that we shall live with Him forever in everlasting innocence, righteousness, and blessedness. We can be thankful that Jesus is master over all our sorrows and griefs.

Isaiah also teaches us to sing, "In that day they will say, 'Surely this is our God; we trusted in him, and he saved us. This is the Lord, we trusted in him; let us rejoice and be glad in his salvation.' " Compared to many people in the world, we have much to be thankful for. But even if we had nothing but the clothes on our backs, we could still say Amen when we pray, because if we have Jesus, we have all we need to live forever. "Forever" is another name for "Amen" — because Jesus is both always there and always true. The world may fall apart around us, but we always have Jesus to see us safely through until we sit with him forever in his eternal kingdom, power, and glory. Jesus is God's Amen to us that the day will come when God will make all we have endured worth it.

So, how can we be thankful when there is so much for which to be unthankful? How can we say Amen, no matter what happens to us? By turning to Jesus, who is the great Amen. Because of Him, we have hope for the future, help in the present, and healing of the past. We can only say Amen because God has said it to us first, through the life, death, and resurrection to life again of the Lord Jesus Christ. As we consider all that Jesus has done for us, we can then be thankful for whatever comes our way, believing that He only sends our way what is good for us.

Prayer: Lord Jesus, Your kingdom, power, and glory are forever and sure. Your eternal government makes it possible for us to say Amen to our prayers because You are God's Amen spoken to us. We are thankful for the salvation You have worked on us. We are also thankful for the countless blessings we enjoy, downpayments of treasure laid up in heaven for us. Forgive us when we grumble about what we don't have or what we have lost. Help us be thankful no matter what happens to us by reminding us of what we have that is forever. Amen.

Exodus 30:17-21
Acts 2:36-40
Matthew 28:16-20

46. Holy Baptism: Washed In God's Name

> **THE SACRAMENT OF HOLY BAPTISM —**
> **THE NATURE OF BAPTISM**
> Baptism is not simple water only, but it is the water comprehended in God's command and connected with God's word. Christ, our Lord, says in the last chapter of Matthew: Go ye and teach all nations, baptizing them in the name of the Father and of the Son and of the Holy Ghost ... [Baptism] works forgiveness of sins, delivers from death and the devil, and gives eternal salvation to all who believe this, as the words and promises of God declare. Christ, our Lord, says in the last chapter of Mark: He that believeth and is baptized shall be saved; but he that believeth not shall be damned.

After Jesus rose from the dead, He sent His disciples on a mission. Jesus told them to make disciples wherever they went. A disciple in the Bible is a student. So, Jesus told His students to make the class bigger by adding more students to it. He also told them how they make disciples of people. At the head of the list is baptism. "Make disciples of all nations, baptizing them in the name of the Father and of the Son and of the Holy Ghost." Baptism is closely connected to Jesus' rising from the dead. Jesus rose from the dead to save us from sin, death, and the power of the devil. Jesus promised that whoever believes and is baptized shall be saved. Baptism somehow makes the resurrection of Jesus from the dead known to us.

First, let's review what it means to baptize someone in the name of the Father and the Son and of the Holy Spirit. To baptize means to wash something. Jesus once pointed out that the Pharisees baptize everything: cups, pitchers, kettles, and recliner chairs. The author of the letter to the Hebrews pointed out that the hand and foot washings of the priests were temporary regulations until the coming of Jesus. Washing happens when you dip something in water. But the thing washed doesn't have to be dipped. Sometimes it is. Sometimes only a washcloth is dipped. Many people wash dishes and the kitchen table with the same washcloth. The dishes were dipped, the table wasn't. Both get baptized, according to the way the word was used in Bible times. The same is also true when we take a bath. You can take a bath in a tub, or in a sink (ever hear of a sponge bath? — nurses give them all the time in hospitals). Christian baptism is a sacred bath. The quantity or depth of water is not the issue. The purpose is the issue.

The purpose of Christian baptism is connected to the name of the Father and of the Son and of the Holy Spirit. We are supposed to make disciples by baptizing people in the name of the Father and of the Son and of the Holy Ghost. Now, we wash clothes in the washing machine. We wash dishes in the sink. We wash ourselves in the shower, the sink, or the bathtub. We wash the car in the driveway or carwash. We baptize in the name of the Father and of the Son and of the Holy Spirit. So the name of God is the place where Christian washing happens. A close look at the name of God, here given in three parts, tells us what will happen in that sacred bath.

The name of the Father is branded on creation. Father is what we call the man who gave life to us and uses his strength to protect and care for us. God the Father is the Maker of heaven and earth. He is our maker, our Father. The name of the Son is branded on the church (we call it the "Christian" church, don't we?). If one is a son, he has a father. Together, that makes a family. The church is the family of God. Jesus is our big brother. God the Son was willing to sacrifice himself to bring and keep the family together. The name of the Spirit is branded on our lives. A spirit is air that moves. The wind keeps the air from getting stale. Wind moves in and out of our bodies to keep our bodies alive. The Holy Spirit gives us life by breathing into us the Word of God that heals the heart and mind and breathing out of us sin and death.

We should not be surprised, then, that Jesus wants us to baptize everyone. Baptism brings a person into the family of God. Baptism joins us to the saving work of Jesus. Baptism gives us a new start in life. For most Christians, this happens very near the beginning of their human lives. That's because we know people are sinful from the moment they are microscopic dots inside their mothers, doomed to die. We know they need to hear the message of forgiveness of sins and eternal life as soon as possible. Baptism acts out the message — we actually see God forgiving sins. That makes baptism a very good teaching tool to use for people who are not ready to learn by listening to Bible stories. That's why we baptize babies or those who are babylike in mental development. For those who learn about Jesus later in life, baptism adds "Amen" to the spoken word.

When water is used according to the command of Jesus, a miracle happens. The water carries to us the cleansing power of God's Word and carries away the dirt of sin. Anyone who is baptized owns a place in God's eternal family. May God grant that we live up to that family name.

Prayer: We thank You, Lord Jesus, that You sent people to make disciples of us, who baptized us. We know that baptism joins us to You and sets us apart from sin, death, and the devil. When we are bothered by shame, remind us that all our sins were washed away at our baptism, even those we had not yet committed. Help us believe that, whether spoken or acted out, as in baptism, Your Word of forgiveness touches our whole life, not just the part we have already lived. Amen.

2 Kings 5:1-3, 9-14
Titus 3:3-7
John 4:46-54

47. Holy Baptism: A Bath That Renews

> **THE SACRAMENT OF HOLY BAPTISM — THE POWER OF BAPTISM**
>
> *How can water do such great things [as forgive sins and give eternal life]?* It is not the water indeed that does them, but the word of God which is in and with the water, and faith, which trusts such word of God in the water. For without the word of God the water is simple water and no Baptism. But with the word of God it is a Baptism, that is, a gracious water of life and a washing of regeneration in the Holy Ghost, as Saint Paul says, Titus, chapter third: [According to His mercy He saved us] By the washing of regeneration and renewing of the Holy Ghost ... It signifies that the Old Adam in us should by daily contrition and repentance, be drowned and die with all sins and evil lusts and, again, a new man daily come forth and arise, who shall live before God in righteousness and purity forever. Saint Paul writes, Romans, chapter sixth: We are buried with Christ by Baptism into death, that, like as He was raised up from the dead by the glory of the Father, even so we also should walk in newness of life.

Scriptures like the one from Paul's letter to the Romans above show the clear connection between the resurrection of Jesus and Christian baptism. By baptism we die and rise to life again with Christ. The Scripture from Paul's letter to Titus shows how this can happen: The Holy Spirit uses baptism to regenerate and renew us. A miracle happens in baptism. This miracle is connected to what God says and does, not what we say and do. In the Old Testament there is a story that illustrates this.

In the land that is today known as Lebanon, but was known as Aram in those days, there was an Aramean army general named Naaman who caught leprosy. This meant the end of his family life, his military career, and all that went with this high position. But God had hidden a surprise in Naaman's war prizes. A little girl he bought as a slave who was captured in a raid on the nation of Israel stepped forward with some good news. She told about a prophet named Elisha in her homeland who could help him. The king of Aram and Naaman were so desperate that the king sent Naaman back to Israel to find the miracle worker. So Naaman went back to Israel to find Elisha. That would be like a general returning to a country he crushed in war to receive cancer treatments! Naaman finally arrived at the home of the famous prophet Elisha.

Naaman expected the man of God to tell Naaman to do some great thing. Maybe he expected Elisha to send him on a pilgrimage. Maybe Naaman expected Elisha to ask Naaman to perform an elaborate religious ritual. Naaman was willing to climb Mount Everest or travel to deepest, darkest Africa if that would earn him the cure he so desperately wanted.

What Naaman got was a major disappointment. Instead of Elisha, a messenger came out of the house. "Go take a bath in the Jordan River and you will be healed." The Jordan! That muddy creek! Imagine that you go to the doctor because you have cancer. But instead of getting to see the doctor, the receptionist comes up to you and says, "Take a bath in the duck pond at the city park and you will be cured." Naaman was furious. "I traveled hundreds of miles. I had to bow before an enemy king and risk my neck to come here. And he sends a slave to tell me to take a bath in the Jordan? Besides, aren't the rivers back home better than any water in this country?"

One of Naaman's slaves finally talked Naaman into taking the bath. His argument was simple. "If the prophet had told you to do some great thing, wouldn't you have done it? How much more, then, when he tells you, wash and be cleansed?" Another way of saying that is, "You'd do something great if he told you, so why not do this easy thing?" Naaman did. Down to the Jordan he went — seven dips in the river. On the seventh dip, the leprosy left. Obviously, it wasn't the water that cured Naaman. This wasn't some kind of miracle water. Six dips in the river only got Naaman wet. It was the seventh dip, according to the word of the prophet, that did the healing. This is how God does things. He speaks His Word, but joins it to something that we can see. Those who take the bath called baptism are cleansed of something worse than leprosy. They are cured of death! How? The water? No, not the water. God's Word in the water does the healing. Faith accepts it. Naaman was not healed until he believed the prophet and took the bath. In a greater way, those who believe that baptism washes away their sins and gives them new life have what God offers.

Prayer: Lord Jesus, help us believe that our sins are forgiven because we have been baptized. Forgive us for seeing only the water and doubting that ordinary water could do such a thing. Help us live like baptized people — people who have died to sin and who have begun a new life that lasts forever, a life like Yours. Help us to repent daily of the sins that try to drag us back into unbelief. Help us to claim daily the heritage and hope that You gave us when we were baptized. Amen.

Exodus 32:1-14
1 Corinthians 3:1-11
John 20:19-23

48. The Office Of The Keys: Why Pastors?

> **THE OFFICE OF THE KEYS AND CONFESSION**
> *What is the Office of the Keys?* It is the peculiar church power which Christ has given to His Church on earth to forgive the sins of penitent sinners, but to retain the sins of the impenitent as long as they do not repent.
>
> *Where is this written?* Thus writes the holy Evangelist John, chapter twentieth: The Lord Jesus breathed on His disciples and saith unto them, Receive ye the Holy Ghost. Whosesoever sins ye remit, they are remitted unto them; and whosesoever sins ye retain, they are retained.
>
> *What do you believe according to these words?* I believe that, when the called ministers of Christ deal with us by His divine command, especially when they exclude manifest and impenitent sinners from the Christian congregation, and, again, when they absolve those who repent of their sins and are willing to amend, this is as valid and certain, in heaven also, as if Christ, our dear Lord, dealt with us Himself.

The story goes that a terrified little boy came running into his father's bedroom during a thunderstorm. Dad told him, "Don't be afraid. You can go back to your room because God is with you." "But," replied the boy anxiously as he continued to burrow into bed next to his father, "I can't see Him, and what I really need now is a God with some skin on Him."

Since the beginning of history, mankind has wanted to see God. Few, however, have laid eyes on God. Adam walked with God in

Eden, but that came to an end when Adam tried to take God's place. Enoch walked with God, but vanished one day, leaving behind no report of what he saw. Moses got to see God's backside. Nebuchadnezzar saw Him briefly in the fiery furnace with Shadrach, Meshach, and Abednego. In the days of the apostles, God became flesh and many people saw Him walk their streets, heal their sick, and finally suffer torture and death on a cross. The rest of humankind, however, has not been so fortunate.

Yet this has not stopped them from coming up with substitutes. In the days of Moses, for example, the people made for themselves a golden calf as a representation of God. This was a common symbol used in worship in those days. Since most people were agricultural, a calf represented life and strength, qualities of God. In the same way that America is pictured as an eagle swooping down on her enemies, people pictured God as different kinds of animals or heroic men.

We know what happened to Israel's attempt to visualize and locate God in some man-made object. What would you think if someone showed you a penny and told you, "This represents America"? What would you think if someone showed you a gold-plated ant and told you that it reminds them how smart and strong you are? In like manner, people's attempts to represent God as animals, or even as heroic men like Hercules or Jupiter, are an insult to Him.

Worse, since idols so grossly lie about God's abilities and work, people who use them are led to believe false things about God. Instead of seeing God as a holy and righteous God who cannot permit evil to endure, idols lead people to think that God can be managed or controlled in some way. That is why God was death on idolatry; which is also why God rolled up His sleeves and told Moses, "Stand aside, I've had it with this stiff-necked people. I'm going to blast them to cinders. Then I'm going to start all over, and raise a new nation from you, Moses."

We know the rest of the story. Moses prayed to God. "Remember the bargain *You* made with the people *You* brought out of Egypt? If You blast them, then people like the Egyptians will say, 'Get a load of this, Jehovah brought His people out of slavery so He could incinerate them in the desert.' " So Moses begged God to forgive the people, and, of course, God did.

This wasn't the first time forgiveness worked this way. When God came down to earth to destroy Sodom and Gomorrah, Abraham pleaded that God would spare one family from the judgment they deserved. So God made sure that Abraham's nephew Lot and his family had a chance to escape. When King David confessed to adultery, murder, and deceit, the prophet Nathan forgave David. Besides this, of course, the whole sacrificial system of the Hebrews constantly proclaimed forgiveness. It is no surprise, then, that the Lord Jesus told His disciples that they were to go about and announce the grace of God, and in His stead, and by His command, they were to forgive the sins of those who repented.

Of course, the apostles did not get the job done of forgiving and retaining sins. So before they died, they trained up men to take their place in this important work. The Bible calls these men "pastors." That's where we are today. We still don't get to see God. But we can have God "with skin on" by going to one of His agents, a pastor.

The word "pastor" means "shepherd." It is related to the word "pasture," the place where sheep go to eat. Think about Psalm 23: "The Lord is my shepherd." We could just as easily say, "The Lord is my pastor." This makes me think of something the Lord Jesus tells us: "I am the good shepherd, the good pastor. I lay down my life for my sheep." Think also what the Lord Jesus said to Peter after He rose from the dead. He took Peter aside and asked him three times, "Do you love me?" Remember what Jesus said when Peter replied each time, "Of course I love you"? He said, "Then feed my sheep, feed my lambs." Jesus, the Good Shepherd, appoints other shepherds to help Him.

How did Peter feed the lambs of Jesus? The people of God had sung answer to that for a thousand years: "The Lord is my shepherd, I shall not want. *He leads me to green pastures; He leads me beside still waters; He restores my soul.*" Jesus fed, watered, and restored Peter's soul by putting him back to work as though Peter had never denied Jesus or sinned against Him. Jesus told Peter to now go and feed, water, and restore the souls of others.

Doesn't that fit the work of a pastor? We come to a pastor, whether in a church service, or the privacy of his office, with a load of guilt and shame that has accumulated. In our prayers before him, we confess to God that we are poor miserable sinners who have sinned against God in thought, word, and deed, by what we have done and by what we have left undone. We admit that we have not loved God with our whole heart and that we have not loved our neighbors as ourselves. We even announce that we justly deserve God's punishment now and forever.

That's when the pastor gets to lead us to green pastures and quiet waters and restore our souls. The green pasture is words like: "Almighty God, our heavenly Father, has had mercy on us and sent his only begotten Son to die for us, and for his sake forgives us all our sins." He restores our souls, saying, "Upon this your confession, as a called and ordained servant of the Word, I therefore forgive you all your sins in the name of the Father and of the Son and of the Holy Spirit" (leading us also by these words back to the quiet waters of baptism, where the name of God was first spoken over us).

It often bothers some people when they first hear a pastor talk this way. They wonder, "How can he say such a thing? Only God can forgive sinners!" This is true. But was it a voice that boomed from heaven that told those who made the golden calf that they were forgiven? Was it a voice from heaven that answered each sacrifice offered with good news that sins were atoned? No, God used human agents, like Moses or the priests. Even when God went to rescue Lot and his family from Sodom and Gomorrah, He did so in human form.

One day, some people brought a paralyzed man to Jesus, hoping He would heal the man. But the first thing Jesus did was to say, "Your sins are forgiven." That caused many people to think, "Who does he think he is? Only *God* can forgive sins." That's when Jesus said, "So that you will know that the Son of Man has power on earth to forgive sins — " He turned to the paralyzed man and said, "Get up and walk." The people then praised God that such authority to forgive sins had been given to *men* on earth. Even Jesus forgave only with authority given to Him from heaven!

So it's not really the pastor who forgives sins, any more than it is the pastor who washes away sins in baptism, nor is it the pastor who offers the body and blood of Jesus in Holy Communion. Only God can do these things. But pastors do these things "in the stead, and by the command" of Jesus. "In the stead" means "in Jesus' place." "By His command" means that Jesus told pastors to do these things. Let's say I hire a lawyer to make a land purchase. I empower him to use his good judgment in arriving at a price. So the lawyer goes to the seller and says, "Okay, this is what I can offer," and he names a price. But who is really making the offer — the lawyer?

The Apostle Paul tells us in his letter to the Ephesians that when Jesus ascended to heaven, He gave gifts to His church, people who would speak for Him in various ways. Included in the list are pastors. Among many responsibilities Jesus gave to pastors, He has handed to each a key, one that can lock or unlock heaven's door to a sinner. The key is simple: with the turn of a few words, a pastor either keeps a sinner out of heaven or lets one in. He has been commanded to keep out those who refuse to give up their sins; but He has been commanded by Jesus to let in those who repent of their sins and are willing to amend their lives.

Prayer: Lord Jesus, we thank You for the gift of pastors and the forgiveness of sins which they offer to us in so many different ways, especially when they announce to us out loud that our sins are forgiven. By Your Spirit, make us always willing to confess our sins and to believe that when one of Your called ministers forgives us, it is as valid and certain in heaven as though You have done it Yourself. Amen.

Joel 2:28-32
Acts 2:1-12
John 20:19-31

49. Confession: Confess And Absolve

> **THE OFFICE OF THE KEYS AND CONFESSION**
> *What is Confession?* Confession embraces two parts. One is that we confess our sins; the other, that we receive absolution, or forgiveness from the pastor as from God Himself, and in no wise doubt but firmly believe that by it our sins are forgiven before God in heaven.
> *What sins shall we confess?* Before God we should plead guilty of all sins, even of those which we do not know, as we do in the Lord's Prayer; but before the pastor we should confess those sins only which we know and feel in our hearts ... Here consider your station according to the Ten Commandments, whether you are a father, mother, son, daughter, master, mistress, servant; whether you have been disobedient, unfaithful, slothful; whether you have grieved any person by word or deed; whether you have stolen, neglected, or wasted aught, or done other injury.

Today we celebrate Pentecost. It's the oldest holiday we celebrate in the church. It's older than Christmas or Easter. It goes back about 3,500 years to the days of Moses. Pentecost was one of four major holidays for God's people in those days. We no longer celebrate Passover because Easter replaced it. We no longer celebrate Atonement Day, for Good Friday replaced that. The Festival of Tabernacles, or Booths, has also faded into the past. Only Pentecost remains. The name Pentecost means "fifty." It comes fifty days after the old Passover. Originally, Pentecost was the spring harvest festival. But Jesus changed Pentecost into a holiday that started the final harvest of souls.

Remember how the disciples of Jesus had gathered on the Pentecost that followed the death and resurrection of Jesus? Remember how suddenly there was the sound of a mighty wind? Remember how fire landed on all the people and they began to speak about Jesus in languages they never learned? Pentecost is a Christian holiday now that celebrates the fact that Jesus has anointed all of God's people with His Holy Spirit. Each Pentecost is like a birthday party for the Christian church. Each of us can celebrate how we are prophets, priests, and kings in the kingdom of heaven. That's because in the old days of the church, before Jesus, the Holy Spirit of God was poured out on only prophets, priests, and kings.

We get an idea of what it means to be prophets, priests, and kings from what happened when Jesus appeared to His disciples on the day He rose from the dead. "On the evening of that first day of the week, when the disciples were together, with the doors locked for fear of the Jews, Jesus came and stood among them and said, 'Peace be with you!' After He said this, He showed them His hands and side. The disciples were overjoyed when they saw the Lord. Again Jesus said, 'Peace be with you! As the Father has sent me, I am sending you.' And with that he breathed on them and said, 'Receive the Holy Spirit. If you forgive anyone his sins, they are forgiven; if you do not forgive them, they are not forgiven.' " Jesus gave His Spirit so that we could proclaim forgiveness of sins. First Jesus blew His Spirit on the Apostles. But, a few weeks later, He blew that same Spirit on all His disciples.

Ever since that time, wherever the name and fame of Jesus Christ have been preached, sinners have prayed for forgiveness. Wherever sinners have prayed for forgiveness, Christians have preached forgiveness of sins. Theologians have given a name to all this: confession. Confession means admitting with each other that we are sinners. It means admitting that we are bad parents, disobedient children, lazy workers, harsh masters. Confession means admitting that we use our mouths as knives to slash and stab people around us. Confession means admitting that we have behaved badly to people around us. Confession means admitting that we lie, cheat, steal, and hurt people around us in many ways. If you have no crimes against God or your fellowman to confess, you are either dead or a hypocrite. But if you can pinch yourself and know that you are alive, and know that you do not obey God's law, then confess it!

Confession also means admitting with each other that Jesus is the only one who can absolve our sins. Absolve means having our sins taken away. It's a rare word used only in the church these days that means the same thing as forgive — loosen and take away. Confession is good for the soul because Jesus stands ready to peel sin from it like old paint from old, worn-out furniture. Once Jesus removes sin, He can then continue with His work of restoration and renewal He started when we were buried with Him in baptism and raised with Him from baptism to new life.

Pentecost celebrates the blessing of confession! Through confession, the Holy Spirit works His healing on us and the world around us. As we confess our sins, the Spirit takes them away for Jesus' sake. As we confess Jesus as our Savior, others hear the good news and can then confess with us.

Prayer: Lord Jesus, Prince of Peace, from whom comes the Holy Spirit, the Giver of life: Help us always to confess our sins and our faith in You. Help us make confession so that others will be attracted to the hope that You offer. Forgive us when we, like hypocrites, don't really think we have much sin to confess. Make our confession pure so we can truly enjoy the forgiveness You offer. Amen.

Exodus 24:1-8
Hebrews 9:15-22
Matthew 26:19-29

50. The Sacrament Of The Altar: Given For You

> **THE SACRAMENT OF THE ALTAR — WHAT THE LORD'S SUPPER IS**
> [The Sacrament of the Altar] is the true body and blood of our Lord Jesus Christ under the bread and wine, for us Christians to eat and to drink, instituted by Christ Himself ... The holy Evangelists Matthew, Mark, Luke, and Paul [the Apostle] write thus: Our Lord Jesus Christ, the same night in which He was betrayed, took bread; and when He had given thanks, He brake it and gave it to His disciples, saying, Take, eat; this is My body, which is given for you. This do in remembrance of Me. After the same manner also He took the cup when He had supped, and when He had given thanks, He gave it to them, saying, Drink ye all of it; this cup is the new testament in My blood, which is shed for you for the remission of sins. This do, as oft as ye drink it, in remembrance of Me.

"Sacrament of the Altar" is one of the names we have for the Lord's Supper, also known as Holy Communion, and the Lord's Table. In our day, the only place we hear of a sacrament is in church. We talk about two sacraments: baptism and the Lord's Supper. A sacrament is a sacred oath, a religious oath. For example, in the days of Jesus, a Roman soldier joined the army by promising his life to serve God and the emperor. The soldier called God as his witness and the soldier pledged his own life to keep the oath. In our day, the closest thing we have to this idea of a "sacrament" in public life is the oath people take in a courtroom, when people lay their hand on a Bible and swear "to tell the truth, the whole truth ... so help me God."

Christians borrowed the word "sacrament" to describe the sacred oath God takes promising His own life that He would forgive our sins. In the sacrament of baptism, the promise of God is acted out by the washing away of sins. In the Lord's Supper, the Sacrament of the Altar, the promise is joined to the death of Jesus.

The letter written to the Hebrews which we have in our Bible helps us understand this. "For this reason Christ is the mediator of a new testament, that those who are called may receive the promised eternal inheritance — now that he has died as a ransom to set them free from the sins committed under the first testament." The Lord's Supper tells us about an inheritance that God promises us.

"In the case of a testament, it is necessary to prove the death of the one who made it, because a testament is in force only when somebody has died; it never takes effect while the one who made it is living." How much proof do we need that Jesus died? Two separate governments were involved in it. In addition, each time we come to the Sacrament of the Altar, we come to hear the reading of the last will and testament of Jesus, something that normally happens only after a person dies. We do not normally bring in the body of "Uncle Joe" to prove that he is really dead. But something like that happens when we go to the Lord's Supper. When we hear the words "My body broken for you" and eat the bread, we take into our mouths the body of Jesus as a reminder that He died. When we drink the wine and hear the words, "My blood shed for you for the forgiveness of sins," we swallow our inheritance, forgiveness, that went into effect after Jesus died.

And 1500 years of priestly activity had predicted all this: "This is why even the first testament was not put into effect without blood. When Moses had proclaimed every commandment of the law to all the people, he took the blood of calves, together with water, scarlet wool, and branches of hyssop, and sprinkled the scroll and all the people. He said, 'This is the blood of the testament, which God has commanded you to keep.' In the same way, he sprinkled with the blood both the tabernacle and everything used in its ceremonies. In fact, the law requires that nearly everything be cleansed with blood, and without the shedding of blood there is no forgiveness." All those calves which were sacrificed stood in for Jesus until He could die the real death of the testament. For centuries, the people saw the death of Jesus acted out in the sacramental death of animals. How blessed we are today to be able to attend the real thing!

Prayer: We thank You, Lord Jesus, for remembering us in Your last will and testament. We also thank You that You have given us a way that the reading of that testament will always be found in the church. When we celebrate Holy Communion, help us believe that we receive what You have promised us in a sacred oath, namely, the forgiveness of sins. Forgive us when we doubt that bread and wine are visible containers of the invisible promise of forgiveness and containers of the supernatural pledge of Your body and blood given as proof that the testament is in effect. Bless those who attend Your sacramental meal with forgiveness and with faith to trust that forgiveness. Amen.

Object lesson: "Given for you." Take three children. Give one an envelope with play money in it. Make one to be a judge. Have him read some court charges out loud to the third child. "By order of this court you have been found guilty of not cleaning your room as you should. Your sentence is that you either pay the court thirty play dollars or spend thirty days cleaning the whole school." Ask him what he plans to do — pay the fine or clean the school. Then whisper to the child with money that he could offer to pay the fine. Tell him to hand the money to the judge and say, "This money is given for (name of person)." Does the person have to pay the fine or clean the schoolhouse now? No. What does "given for you" mean? Given by someone else as though you gave it, in your place, to your credit. How does Jesus give Himself for us to forgive our sins? We owe our lives to pay for our sins; Jesus paid for us.

Zechariah 9:9-11
1 Corinthians 10:15-17
Matthew 27:22-25

51. The Sacrament Of The Altar: Eat And Drink Forgiveness

> **THE SACRAMENT OF THE ALTAR —**
> **THE BENEFITS AND POWER OF THE LORD'S SUPPER**
> *What is the benefit of such eating and drinking?* That is shown us by these words, "Given and shed for you for the remission of sins"; namely, that in the Sacrament forgiveness of sins, life, and salvation are given us through these words. For where there is forgiveness of sins, there is also life and salvation ... It is not the eating and drinking indeed that does them, but the words here written, "Given and shed for you for the remission of sins"; which words, besides the bodily eating and drinking, are the chief thing in the Sacrament; and he that believes these words has what they say and express, namely, the forgiveness of sins.

The Lord's Supper is very closely connected with the resurrection of Jesus from the dead. I know we usually think of the connection the Lord's Supper has with the death of Jesus, but remember that Jesus tells us that his body and blood are offered to us to eat and drink with the bread and wine. Don't we believe that the body of Jesus is alive today? And didn't Jesus promise to be with us always, until the end of the age? The good news is that one of the ways Jesus Christ is present with us is in the Lord's Supper. As the Apostle Paul points out in his first letter to the Corinthians, "Is not the cup of thanksgiving for which we give thanks a communion in the blood of Christ? And is not the bread that we break a communion in the body of Christ?" In the word "communion" is the word "common." The bread we eat is in common with the body of Jesus. Likewise the wine. Wherever Jesus, according to

His human nature, is found, we also find Him forgiving sins. We should not be surprised that those who eat the Lord's Supper are offered forgiveness of sins.

The key words in the testament of Jesus are these: "Given and shed for you for the remission of sins." To get an idea of what this means, let's listen to what the enemies of Jesus said at His trial before Pontius Pilate. Remember how Pilate was ready to let Jesus go? Pilate could not find anything wrong with Jesus. And Pilate was looking for something wrong. Pilate was very sensitive to anything that smelled like rebellion. The last thing he wanted was some religious nut running around claiming he was the king who would lead the Jews to freedom. Yet Pilate found Jesus harmless. But the enemies of Jesus pressed Pilate for a guilty verdict and a death sentence on Jesus. That's when Pilate realized that a riot would start if he didn't condemn Jesus. So he declared himself innocent of the blood of Jesus. The people, in turn, cried out, "His blood be on us, and on our children."

We know that blood is one of the ways the Bible talks about death. When Pilate said he was innocent of the blood of Jesus, he was trying to deny responsibility for the death of Jesus. The mob, in turn, was willing to take that responsibility. "His blood be on us, and on our children" means "His death is a family matter to us." Little did they know how these words would come true. God answered their prayer by accepting the death of Jesus in their place. The mob was willing to accept responsibility for the death of Jesus. God did them one better. He made Jesus responsible for their deaths. Little did they know that by executing Jesus, they were putting into effect the terms of the last will and testament of Jesus, that His body and blood would be given and shed for the remission of sins!

Now, if I leave my wife 100,000 dollars in my will, and then she poisons my spaghetti, no court worth anything will allow her to get a dime of the inheritance. The Jews took responsibility for the death of Jesus. So they should be disqualified for any benefit that would come from it. The same would also be true for anyone who, like those Jews, thinks that Jesus is a curse. Even we would be disqualified from benefiting from the death of Jesus because apart from what change the Spirit of God has worked in us, we would kill Jesus if we could. We are, at best, accessories to the murder of Jesus.

How strange and wonderful, then, that God allows us to benefit from murdering Jesus! And to show how God has changed that brutal murder into glorious blessing, we have the Lord's Supper. The nail-pierced body of Jesus streaked with blood from the torture He endured is miraculously transformed into a family meal that offers forgiveness. Instead of seeing the brutality of Jesus' death, we see the Father in heaven feeding us forgiveness. It's the same body and blood. But it has been turned into a declaration of forgiveness instead of evidence against us. Saint Paul said it: "As often as you eat this bread and drink this cup you do proclaim the Lord's death until he comes."

Those who take Jesus at His Word and come often to the true Supper He serves have the assurance of forgiveness that Jesus offers there added to the solid declaration of forgiveness made in baptism and which is repeated over and over in the preaching of forgiveness. The Lord knows how much we need to hear that good news. The Lord's Supper is His personal way of declaring it to us.

Prayer: We thank and praise You, Lord Jesus, for the miracle You work each time we come to the Table You set for us. Since only those who believe Your words "given and shed for you for forgiveness" receive forgiveness, give us faith to believe, even though our minds may not understand how You do it. Bless us, according to Your Word, when we come to Your Supper. Amen.

Jeremiah 31:31-34
1 Corinthians 11:23-33
John 13:18-30

52. The Sacrament Of The Altar: The Worthy Dinner Guest

> **THE SACRAMENT OF THE ALTAR —**
> **THE SALUTARY USE OF THE LORD'S SUPPER**
> *Who, then, receives [the Lord's Supper] worthily?* Fasting and bodily preparation are indeed a fine outward training; but he is truly worthy and well prepared who has faith in these words, "Given and shed for you for the remission of sins." But he that does not believe these words, or doubts, is unworthy and unprepared; for the words "for you" require all hearts to believe.

When it comes to making disciples, we will baptize just about anybody, and we will take time to teach anyone about Jesus who is willing to listen. But we don't allow just anyone to come to the Lord's Supper. Many Christians from other churches are bothered by that. A friend of mine was at a church once where a non-Lutheran visitor went up for Communion and the pastor did not give it to him. A few days later, the pastor received a letter from the man's mother blasting him for being unchristian. Many church members have been a bit embarrassed because they brought a friend to church with them on a Communion Sunday and then had to leave the friend behind while the members came forward. Yet there is something wonderful and special about the Lord's Supper that helps us understand why we must be careful about whom we serve it to.

We get our practice from what the Apostle Paul told the church at Corinth. First, he reminded them why the Lord's Supper is celebrated, that Jesus Christ set it up as a way to proclaim the benefits of His death. Saint Paul taught that the Lord's Supper told the message of salvation by showing the death of Jesus in a special way: "For whenever you eat this bread and drink this cup, you proclaim the Lord's death until he comes." Then he added this warning: "Therefore, whoever eats the bread or drinks the cup of the Lord in an unworthy manner will be guilty of sinning against the body and blood of the Lord." The Romans and Jews who crucified Jesus were guilty of sinning against the body and blood of Jesus. To go to Communion in an unworthy manner puts one in the same group as those murderers of our Lord! That is why the apostle adds this advice: "A man ought to examine himself before he eats of the bread and drinks of the cup. For anyone who eats and drinks without recognizing the body of the Lord eats and drinks judgment on himself. That is why many among you are weak and sick, and a number of you have fallen asleep. But if we judged ourselves, we would not come under judgment."

Notice, the apostle warns that it is possible to get hurt by eating the Lord's Supper in an unworthy manner. It's that warning that makes us sit up and take notice. He warns that those who do not discern that the body of Jesus is present, that those who eat the bread as though it were nothing more than bread, would be found liable for the suffering and death of Jesus. He pointed out that many in that church had gotten sick and some had died because they abused the Lord's Supper.

What is it that makes a person worthy to come to the Lord's Supper? The main requirement is a proper faith. It is not confirmation that makes one worthy — though we do have a good reason for doing this. It is also not enough to believe in Jesus. It's also not enough that we share a common faith in the teachings of Jesus, though that is necessary before we can join at the same altar. That kind of faith is enough to qualify as a disciple. It is enough to make one fit for heaven. Worthiness is not based on behavior, either. Jesus doesn't expect us to quit sinning before we come to His Supper. The Lord's Supper is meant for sinners! Remember, it offers forgiveness of sins.

Worthiness is based on faith in the words, "given and shed for you for the forgiveness of sins." The faith Jesus wants us to have to receive the blessings offered in the Lord's Supper in a worthy manner is to believe that when we eat the bread and wine He serves, it carries to us his body and blood, and along with them the forgiveness of sins. Saint Paul warns that it is dangerous, even fatal, to forget what is in and with the bread and wine.

So, all through the ages, the church has been careful to give the Lord's Supper only to those who confess that they are sinners and who believe that Jesus forgives them when they eat His body and blood as offered in the Lord's Supper. Since the pastors are placed in congregations by Jesus Christ to make sure the secret things of God are used properly, churches have always allowed pastors to determine who is ready to receive the body and blood of Jesus in a worthy manner. The test pastors have always used is based on the words of Paul: "A man ought to examine himself before he eats of the bread and drinks of the cup." Confirmation classes and ceremonies are one way pastors have announced that they believe a person can examine himself, but confirmations are not necessary. Some churches only find out if a person can examine himself properly before allowing him to come to the Lord's Supper. When a person can accurately confess what Jesus wants him to believe about sin and forgiveness as offered in the Lord's Supper, then the pastor can allow the person to come to the Lord's Supper.

Remember, the whole purpose of the Lord's Supper is for Jesus to give you forgiveness. Those who don't believe forgiveness is offered, or who think that the meal is only a memorial, would be rejecting the very forgiveness they need — and that's not safe. But instead of focusing on the warning, focus on the miracle that lies behind the warning. Jesus wants people to come to His Supper. "Come to me all you who labor and are heavy laden, and I will give you rest," Jesus tells us, and his Supper is one of the ways He gives rest to us. The warning is there to show us how serious and wonderful that Supper is. If you have sin in your life and believe that Jesus offers you His body and blood in that Supper to forgive you, you may eat of it in a worthy manner. Worthiness is not based on how well we behave, but on how much we believe Jesus and His testament.

One last point: Jesus makes us worthy to come to His Supper. He gives us the faith we need as we learn from Him — another reason why many churches have a long teaching and training program before allowing people to come to the Supper. He gives us His Holy Spirit to help us believe His promises. Those who take Jesus at His Word will find they are worthy to come to His holy meal.

Prayer: Lord Jesus, give us the faith that enables us to come as worthy guests to Your Supper of forgiveness. Help us to believe all You have taught, especially that You offer Your body and blood in that Supper to forgive the sins of those who eat them in the bread and wine. We are not worthy by our own merits, but only by what You work in us. Make us worthy so we can be blessed by this meal when we come to it. Help us teach this truth to those Christians who do not yet discern Your body in that meal, starting with those in our congregation, as well as our Christian neighbors from other churches, so that we may all be able to come to Your Supper together in this life instead of waiting until the next. For Your name's sake we pray. Amen.

Appendix
Hymns For Use With Sermons

Sermon 1	The First Commandment: Eyes On Jesus	
TLH 244	Glory Be to God the Father	LW 173
TLH 38	The Lord, My God, Be Praised	LW 174
TLH 239	Come, Thou Almighty King	LW 169
TLH 250	Holy God, We Praise Thy Name	LW 171
Sermon 2	The Second Commandment: God's Name	
TLH 457	What A Friend We Have in Jesus	LW 516
TLH 456	Approach, My Soul, the Mercy Seat	
TLH 339	All Hail the Power of Jesus' Name	LW 272
Sermon 3	The Third Commandment: Holding God's Word Sacred	
TLH 4	God Himself Is Present	LW 206
TLH 489	Lord of the Church, We Humbly Pray	LW 261
TLH 285	How Precious Is the Book Divine	LW 332
	Thy Strong Word	LW 328
TLH 10	This is the Day the Lord Hath Made	LW 200
Sermon 4	The Fourth Commandment: Holding Parents In Love And Esteem	
TLH 421	Come, Follow Me, the Savior Spake	LW 379
TLH 625	Oh, Blest the House, Whate'er Befall	LW 467
TLH 417	How Can I Thank Thee, Lord	LW 385
	Our Father, By Whose Name	LW 465
TLH 309	O Jesus, Blessed Lord, to Thee	LW 245
Sermon 5	The Fifth Commandment: Help And Befriend	
TLH 439	O God of Mercy, God of Might	LW 397
TLH 442	Lord of Glory, Who Hast Bought Us	LW 402
TLH 53	Abide, O Dearest Jesus	LW 287
Sermon 6	The Sixth Commandment: A Chaste And Decent Life	
TLH 226	Come, Oh, Come, Thou Quick'ning Spirit	LW 165
TLH 624	O Blessed Home Where Man and Wife	LW 466
TLH 412	May We Thy Precepts, Lord, Fulfill	LW 389
	Son of God, Eternal Savior	LW 394
TLH 234	Holy Ghost, With Light Divine	LW 166

Sermon 7	The Seventh Commandment: Improve And Protect	
TLH 97	Let Us All With Gladsome Voice	LW 42
TLH 425	All Depends on Our Possessing	LW 415
TLH 430	What Is the World to Me	LW 418

Sermon 8	The Eighth Commandment: Speak Well of Your Neighbor	
TLH 652	I Lay My Sins on Jesus	LW 366
TLH 342	Chief of Sinners Though I Be	LW 285
TLH 317	Alas, My God, My Sins Are Great	LW 232
TLH 320	Lord Jesus, Think on Me	LW 231

Sermon 9	The Ninth Commandment: Help And Be Of Service	
TLH 613	Jerusalem the Golden	LW 309
TLH 660	I'm But a Stranger Here	LW 515
TLH 618	Jerusalem, My Happy Home	LW 307

Sermon 10	The Tenth Commandment: Satisfaction	
TLH 439	O God of Mercy, God of Might	LW 397
TLH 196	I Am Content! My Jesus Liveth Still	LW 145
	God of Grace and God of Glory	LW 398
TLH 50	Lord, Dismiss Us With Thy Blessing	LW 218

Sermon 11	The Close Of The Commandments: Grace And Every Blessing	
TLH 609	Wake, Awake, for Night is Flying	LW 177
TLH 279	Today Thy Mercy Calls Us	LW 347
TLH 384	Oh, How Great is Thy Compassion	LW 364

Sermon 12	The First Article: God Gave Me My Eyes And Ears	
TLH 23	Hallelujah! Let Praises Ring	LW 437
TLH 43	We Sing the Almighty Power of God	LW 441
TLH 60	Hark, A Thrilling Voice is Sounding	LW 18
TLH 55	Come, Thou Precious Ransom, Come	LW 34

Sermon 13	The First Article: God Provides For Me	
TLH 39	Praise to the Lord, the Almighty	LW 444
TLH 572	Praise to God, Immortal Praise	LW 496
TLH 25	I Will Sing My Maker's Praises	LW 439
	All Creatures of Our God and King	LW 436
TLH 549	God, Who Madest Earth and Heaven	LW 492

Sermon 14	*The First Article: God's Fatherly, Divine Goodness And Mercy*	
TLH 246	Holy, Holy, Holy	LW 168
TLH 264	Preserve Thy Word, O Savior	LW 337
TLH 68	The Advent of Our King	LW 12
TLH 97	Let Us All With Gladsome Voice	LW 42
Sermon 15	*The First Article: My Duty To Thank And Praise*	
TLH 384	Oh, How Great is Thy Compassion	LW 364
TLH 400	Take My Life and Let It Be	LW 404
TLH 35	Songs of Praise the Angels Sang	LW 447
	Here, O My Lord, I See You Face to Face	LW 243
Sermon 16	*The Second Article: Begotten Of The Father From Eternity*	
TLH 341	Crown Him With Many Crowns	LW 278
TLH 76	A Great and Mighty Wonder	LW 51
TLH 98	Of the Father's Love Begotten	LW 36
TLH 47	Savior, Again to Thy Dear Name We Raise	LW 221
Sermon 17	*The Second Article: Jesus Born Of The Virgin Mary Is My Lord*	
TLH 92	Now Sing We, Now Rejoice	LW 47
TLH 354	In the Cross of Christ I Glory	LW 101
TLH 91	Let the Earth Now Praise the Lord	LW 33
TLH 351	Love Divine, All Love Excelling	LW 286
Sermon 18	*The Second Article: Jesus Is My Lord*	
TLH 76	A Great and Mighty Wonder	LW 51
TLH 80	All Praise to Thee, Eternal God	LW 35
TLH 85	From Heav'n Above to Earth I Come	LW 37
	Once In Royal David's City	LW 58
TLH 55	Come, Thou Precious Ransom, Come	LW 34
Sermon 19	*The Second Article: Jesus Christ Redeemed Me*	
TLH 352	O Savior, Precious Savior	LW 282
TLH 355	Thou Art the Way; to Thee Alone	LW 283
TLH 114	Jesus! Name of Wondrous Love	LW 182
Sermon 20	*The Second Article: Lost And Condemned*	
TLH 367	Hail, Thou Once Despisèd Jesus	LW 284
TLH 360	Oh, For a Thousand Tongues to Sing	LW 276
TLH 417	How Can I Thank Thee, Lord	LW 385
	Christ Is the World's Redeemer	LW 271
TLH 55	Come, Thou Precious Ransom, Come	LW 34

Sermon 21	*The Second Article: Jesus Purchased And Won Me*	
TLH 344	Come, Let Us Join Our Cheerful Songs	LW 204
TLH 175	When I Survey the Wondrous Cross	LW 114
TLH 172	O Sacred Head, Now Wounded	LW 113
	My Song Is Love Unknown	LW 91
TLH 149	Come to Calvary's Holy Mountain	LW 96
Sermon 22	*The Second Article: Protected From The Devil's Power*	
TLH 324	Jesus Sinners Doth Receive	LW 229
TLH 367	Hail, Thou Once Despisèd Jesus	LW 284
TLH 339	All Hail the Power of Jesus' Name	LW 272
TLH 361	O Jesus, King Most Wonderful	LW 274
Sermon 23	*The Second Article: A New Purpose In Life*	
TLH 394	My Faith Looks Up to Thee	LW 378
TLH 390	Drawn to the Cross	LW 356
TLH 376	Rock of Ages, Cleft for Me	LW 361
TLH 401	Praise to Thee and Adoration	LW 387
Sermon 24	*The Second Article: God's Power Takes Care Of Me*	
TLH 161	Hosanna, Loud Hosanna	LW 106
TLH 160	All Glory, Laud, and Honor	LW 102
TLH 361	O Jesus, King Most Wonderful	LW 274
TLH 55	Come, Thou Precious Ransom, Come	LW 34
TLH 309	O Jesus, Blessed Lord, to Thee	LW 245
Sermon 25	*The Second Article: Risen From The Dead*	
TLH 205	The Day of Resurrection	LW 133
TLH 187	Christ is Arisen	LW 124
TLH 208	Ye Sons and Daughters of the King	LW 130
TLH 192	Awake, My Heart, with Gladness	LW 128
	Now All the Vault of Heaven Resounds	LW 131
TLH 202	Welcome, Happy Morning	LW 135
Sermon 26	*The Second Article: What Jesus Does For Us Today*	
TLH 201	Jesus Lives! The Victory's Won	LW 139
TLH 187	Christ is Arisen	LW 124
TLH 361	O Jesus, King Most Wonderful	LW 274
TLH 339	All Hail the Power of Jesus' Name	LW 272
	With High Delight Let Us Unite	LW 134
TLH 189	He Is Arisen! Glorious Word!	LW 520

Sermon 27	The Third Article: Called By The Gospel	
TLH 66	Hark the Glad Sound!	LW 29
TLH 132	O God of God, O Light of Light	LW 83
TLH 134	Songs of Thankfulness and Praise	LW 88
TLH 261	Lord, Keep Us Steadfast in Thy Word	LW 334

Sermon 28	The Third Article: Enlightened With His Gifts	
TLH 294	O Word of God Incarnate	LW 335
TLH 298	Baptized Into Thy Name Most Holy	LW 224
TLH 285	How Precious Is the Book Divine	LW 332
TLH 52	Almighty Father, Bless the Word	LW 216

Sermon 29	The Third Article: Sanctified And Kept In Faith	
TLH 421	Come, Follow Me, the Savior Spake	LW 379
TLH 439	O God of Mercy, God of Might	LW 397
TLH 403	Savior, Thy Dying Love	LW 374
TLH 395	O God, Thou Faithful God	LW 371

Sermon 30	The Third Article: He Calls, Gathers, Enlightens The Whole Church	
TLH 465	Christ Is Our Cornerstone	LW 290
TLH 469	Glorious Things of Thee Are Spoken	LW 294
TLH 462	I Love Thy Kingdom, Lord	LW 296
TLH 464	Blest Be the Tie That Binds	LW 295

Sermon 31	The Third Article: Rich And Daily Forgiveness	
TLH 279	Today Thy Mercy Calls Us	LW 347
TLH 388	Just As I Am, Without One Plea	LW 359
TLH 342	Chief of Sinners Though I Be	LW 285
TLH 371	Jesus, Thy Blood and Righteousness	LW 362
TLH 309	O Jesus, Blessed Lord, to Thee	LW 245

Sermon 32	The Third Article: Raise Up Me And All The Dead	
TLH 130	O Jesus, King of Glory	LW 79
TLH 196	I Am Content! My Jesus Liveth Still	LW 145
TLH 205	The Day of Resurrection	LW 133
TLH 371	Jesus, Thy Blood and Righteousness	LW 362

Sermon 33	The Third Article: God's Gift Of Eternal Life	
TLH 127	As With Gladness Men of Old	LW 75
TLH 656	Behold a Host, Arrayed in White	LW 192
TLH 463	For All the Saints	LW 191
	When Morning Gilds the Skies	LW 460
TLH 613	Jerusalem the Golden	LW 309

Sermon 34	*The Lord's Prayer — The Introduction: Our Father In Heaven*	
TLH 459	Come, My Soul, Thy Suit Prepare	LW 433
TLH 458	Our Father, Thou in Heaven Above	LW 431
TLH 244	Glory Be to God the Father	LW 173
Sermon 35	*The Lord's Prayer — The First Petition: Hallowed Be Thy Name*	
TLH 296	Speak, O Lord, Thy Servant Heareth	LW 339
TLH 458	Our Father, Thou in Heaven Above	LW 431
TLH 439	O God of Mercy, God of Might	LW 397
TLH 360	Oh, for a Thousand Tongues to Sing	LW 276
Sermon 36	*The Lord's Prayer — The Second Petition: Thy Kingdom Come*	
TLH 511	Jesus Shall Reign Where'er the Sun	LW 312
TLH 458	Our Father, Thou in Heaven Above	LW 431
TLH 512	O Christ, Our True and Only Light	LW 314
Sermon 37	*The Lord's Prayer — The Third Petition: Thy Will Be Done*	
TLH 517	The Will of God is Always Best	LW 425
TLH 458	Our Father, Thou in Heaven Above	LW 431
TLH 514	God Moves in a Mysterious Way	LW 426
TLH 529	I Leave All Things to God's Direction	LW 429
TLH 535	Rejoice, My Heart, Be Glad and Sing	LW 424
Sermon 38	*The Lord's Prayer — The Fourth Petition: Give Us This Day Our Daily Bread*	
TLH 430	What Is the World to Me	LW 418
TLH 458	Our Father, Thou in Heaven Above	LW 431
TLH 572	Praise to God, Immortal Praise	LW 496
Sermon 39	*The Lord's Prayer — The Fifth Petition: Forgive Us Our Trespasses*	
TLH 250	Holy God, We Praise Thy Name	LW 171
	Thy Strong Word	LW 328
TLH 458	Our Father, Thou in Heaven Above	LW 431
TLH 387	Dear Christians, One and All, Rejoice	LW 353
Sermon 40	*The Lord's Prayer — The Sixth Petition: Lead Us Not Into Temptation*	
TLH 361	O Jesus, King Most Wonderful	LW 274
TLH 458	Our Father, Thou in Heaven Above	LW 431
TLH 457	What a Friend We Have in Jesus	LW 516

Sermon 41	*The Lord's Prayer — The Seventh Petition: Deliver Us From Evil*	
TLH 428	I Am Trusting Thee, Lord Jesus	LW 408
TLH 458	Our Father, Thou in Heaven Above	LW 431
TLH 429	Lord, Thee I Love with All My Heart	LW 413
TLH 425	All Depends on Our Possessing	LW 415
TLH 427	How Firm a Foundation	LW 411
Sermon 42	*The Lord's Prayer — The Conclusion: Thine Is The Kingdom*	
TLH 360	Oh, For a Thousand Tongues to Sing	LW 276
TLH 458	Our Father, Thou in Heaven Above	LW 431
TLH 341	Crown Him with Many Crowns	LW 278
Sermon 43	*The Lord's Prayer — The Conclusion: Thine Is The Power*	
TLH 352	O Savior, Precious Savior	LW 282
TLH 458	Our Father, Thou in Heaven Above	LW 431
TLH 298	Baptized into Thy Name Most Holy	LW 224
TLH 262	A Mighty Fortress Is Our God	LW 297
Sermon 44	*The Lord's Prayer — The Conclusion: Thine Is The Glory*	
TLH 294	O Word of God Incarnate	LW 335
TLH 458	Our Father, Thou in Heaven Above	LW 431
TLH 297	The Gospel Shows the Father's Grace	LW 330
	Thy Strong Word	LW 328
TLH 309	O Jesus, Blessed Lord, to Thee	LW 245
Sermon 45	*The Lord's Prayer — The Conclusion: Amen*	
TLH 263	O Little Flock, Fear Not the Foe	LW 300
TLH 458	Our Father, Thou in Heaven Above	LW 431
TLH 572	Praise to God, Immortal Praise	LW 496
Sermon 46	*Holy Baptism: Washed In God's Name*	
TLH 298	Baptized Into Thy Name Most Holy	LW 224
	On Galilee's High Mountain	LW 320
TLH 428	I Am Trusting Thee, Lord Jesus	LW 408
TLH 361	O Jesus, King Most Wonderful	LW 274
Sermon 47	*Holy Baptism: A Bath That Renews*	
TLH 334	Let Me Be Thine Forever	LW 257
TLH 338	Thine Forever, God of Love	LW 256
TLH 288	Lord, Help Us Ever to Retain	LW 477
TLH 309	O Jesus, Blessed Lord, to Thee	LW 245

Sermon 48	*The Office Of The Keys: Why Pastors?*	
TLH 426	The Lord My Shepherd Is	
	The Lord's My Shepherd, Leading Me	LW 417
TLH 487	How Beauteous Are Their Feet	
	Preach You the Word	LW 259
TLH 483	God of the Prophets,	
	Bless the Prophets' Sons	LW 258
TLH 489	Lord of the Church, We Humbly Pray	LW 261
Sermon 49	*Confession: Confess And Absolve*	
TLH 233	Come, Holy Ghost, Creator Blest	LW 158
TLH 234	Holy Ghost, with Light Divine	LW 166
TLH 324	Jesus Sinners Doth Receive	LW 229
TLH 309	O Jesus, Blessed Lord, to Thee	LW 245
Sermon 50	*The Sacrament Of The Altar: Given For You*	
TLH 193	Christ the Lord is Risen Today	LW 142
TLH 316	O Living Bread from Heaven	LW 244
TLH 307	Draw Nigh and Take the Body of the Lord	LW 240
TLH 309	O Jesus, Blessed Lord, to Thee	LW 245
Sermon 51	*The Sacrament Of The Altar: Eat And Drink Forgiveness*	
TLH 311	Jesus Christ, Our Blessed Savior	LW 236
TLH 315	I Come, O Savior, to Thy Table	LW 242
TLH 310	Your Table I Approach	LW 249
	Let All Mortal Flesh Keep Silence	LW 241
TLH 309	O Jesus, Blessed Lord, To Thee	LW 245
Sermon 52	*The Sacrament Of The Altar: The Worthy Dinner Guest*	
TLH 312	Lord Jesus Christ, Thou Living Bread	LW 248
TLH 305	Soul, Adorn Thyself With Gladness	LW 239
TLH 309	O Jesus, Blessed Lord, to Thee	LW 245

www.ingramcontent.com/pod-product-compliance
Lightning Source LLC
Chambersburg PA
CBHW071155160426
43196CB00011B/2084